HOW TO SELL YOUR HOME FAST

The American Homeowners Foundation
Arlington, Virginia

Copyright 1994 by the

American Homeowners Foundation

Arlington, VA

All rights reserved.

Owners of this book may reproduce worksheets contained herein for their personal use only. With that exception, reproduction or translation of any part of this work beyond that permitted by Section 107 or 108 of the 1976 United States Copyright Act without the permission of the copyright owner is unlawful. Requests for permission or further information should be addressed to The American Homeowners Foundation.

This publication is designed to provide accurate and authoritative information in regard to the subject matter covered. It is sold with the understanding that the publisher is not engaged in rendering legal, accounting, or other professional services. If legal advice or other expert assistance is required, the services of a competent professional person should be sought. FROM A DECLARATION OF PRINCIPLES JOINTLY ADOPTED BY A COMMITTEE OF THE AMERICAN BAR ASSOCIATION AND A COMMITTEE OF PUBLISHERS.

ISBN 0-940313-09-X

Printed in the United States of America

HOW TO SELL YOUR HOME FAST

THE HOME SELLERS PLAN

TABLE OF CONTENTS

Introduction	page 5
1. Should you Sell?	page 11
2. Shining the Apple	page 23
3. Setting the Price	page 37
4. Selling Your Home: How to Get a Good Broker or How to Market It Yourself	page 45
5. Negotiating	page 71
6. Financing	page 85
7. The Closing	page 95
8. Glossary	page 101
9. Other Resources Available From the American Homeowners Foundation	page 127

HOW TO SELL YOUR HOME FAST

FORWARD

The secret to selling your home in a very slow real estate market is that there is no secret. There is no single "silver bullet" that will assure that your home will be sold in a very short time. The closest thing to a surefire way to sell your house quickly in a slow market is to price it well below the current fair market (and probably depressed) price. That is probably not a viable option for homeowners with limited equity in their homes and not a pleasant prospect for any homeowner.

There are, however, a variety of thoughtful careful steps that homeowners can take to assure that their home will be more likely to sell. The first and most important is to price it realistically. Do not let yourself be influenced by what prices were in the best of times. Price it to be competitive (preferably very competitive) with prices asked for similar homes on the market now.

Make the home shine (see chapter 2). It should look its best both inside and out. Consider minor cost effective steps and even some major cost effective remodeling if you're in a financial position to do so.

Play an active role in developing and executing a market plan. In good times people with a knack for marketing can often market their home effectively without a real estate broker. It's a very iffy proposition in a very slow market. Lack of exposure in the local multiple listing service puts you at a great disadvantage. There are simply too many hungry real estate

HOW TO SELL YOUR HOME FAST
••

agents chasing too few buyers to make such an alternative very viable. A recent alternative -- discount real estate brokers -- offers a cost saving compromise. With some caveats, they offer access to a very powerful marketing tool -- the local multiple listing service. Even if you are using a full service broker, you should be heavily involved in the marketing process -- from the selection of the agent to supplemental marketing techniques to enhance the likelihood of your success.

HOW TO SELL YOUR HOME FAST!

INTRODUCTION

As we enter the 1990s the economy in most of the country is slowing down. With the slowdown, home values in most areas have also stabilized or in some cases have declined. There are some exceptions -- but in many of those cases recent home appreciation is only making up for regionalized stagnation those areas experienced in recent years. After this prior decade's rapid appreciation in housing -- up to 30% per year in some cases, the reversal has come as a rude surprise to many homeowners. In most cases it has been the more expensive homes that have suffered the most. In many cases where the higher priced homes have really taken a beating, the more modest homes have been only moderately affected.

The surprise has been the rudest to those who have recently decided to sell their home for any number of reasons. Many have looked on with satisfaction in recent years as homes in their neighborhood continued to fetch higher and higher prices. Many were counting on banking much of the apparent appreciation, or using it for their childrens' college education, retirement, a second home, investment, or other applications.

For those people who have experienced a recent 10-20% decline in their home's value, the loss of equity must truly appear a disaster. Well, in some cases it is. But in others, believe it or not, it may be a blessing in disguise. In the latter category are most of those with equity remaining despite the decline in their home's value, and who plan to purchase another home of equal or greater value.

Why will they come out even, or maybe ahead? Because the price of the replacement home they will buy will be similarly reduced. Granted, these folks won't take as much equity out of their current home, but the size of their next home loan will be reduced by the same or an even greater amount. In effect, all they'll miss is the opportunity to pay interest on a larger mortgage on their next home.

They will also miss higher commission and closing costs at both the selling and buying ends. Since these together may exceed 10% of a home's price, a decline in home values can significantly reduce these costs. More importantly these are usually cash costs, items that cannot be conveniently folded into the loan on the new home. Of course, homeowners will also benefit from lower real estate taxes on their replacement home, since they will also be less.

And the wisdom of taking equity out of your home when you replace residences is a matter for debate under today's tax laws anyway. When individual tax rates were reduced in 1986, the value of the home interest deduction was also reduced. From a purely economic standpoint, unless you can earn the same interest you would be paying on the mortgage or have a truly pressing need for the cash, you're probably better off with lower home prices anyway.

While there most definitely remain some serious challenges to selling your home in today's market, sellers in this category should take heart at the many offsetting benefits they may not have considered. Some sellers are not so fortunate. Among them are recent buyers who have seen their equity disappear through the decline in home values (especially those without enough extra for a down payment on their next home after they pay off selling costs and the loan on their present home). Also at a disadvantage are those who plan to buy a less expensive home, typically "empty nesters" or divorcees, because their replacement home will likely not have declined in price as much as the one they are selling. Similarly affected are retirees who plan next to rent or move into retirement communities, where values have not declined in many cases.

Perhaps those in the worst position are those who must move for one reason or another and who do not have enough cash and equity to cover all the costs associated with the sale. For them there is no easy answer. They should certainly read this book carefully in order to maximize their potential selling price (and there are other excellent books on selling your home listed in the bibliography). The fact remains that for some, even after taking every possible wise step to maximize their realistic selling price, there will still be a shortfall. Sadly, for them the best course will be to rent out their present home until the market improves and/or consult an attorney familiar with handling personal financial difficulties.

The basic principles of selling a home under slow conditions are the same as selling them in good economic times. However, the importance of taking every possible step to maximize the selling price and minimize the time on the market are much greater. In a strong market even a home that is not in the best of shape and not marketed in the best fashion may sell fairly quickly. In a slow market you can take all the right steps and it can still take a long time to sell. If you don't take all the right steps it may not sell at all (or at least until the market recovers).

Homeowners in particularly slow markets can also consider another option -- renting out their home until the market recovers. While other homeowners with the same thought can also drive the rental rates down, many can more than cover their monthly payments with the rental income. As long as they have or can borrow the necessary down payment if they plan to purchase a replacement, this is an option that can work for some people.

Such an alternative can also yield a tax advantage -- rental homes can be depreciated over 32 years. This means that about 3% of the value of the home (but not the land on which it sits) can be deducted annually from your federal taxable income. This approach can also include a marketing component. Many owners will lease with an option to buy at a fixed price or at a fair market price to be determined by an independent appraisal.

Typically such an arrangement will offer both financial incentives and penalties to the tenant. For example, in a situation where the fair market rent is $1,000 per month, the lease might call for a $1,200 per month rent, with $400 per month credited towards a downpayment if the tenant buys. If the tenant exercises the option to buy, the landlord is basically chipping in $200 per month to the tenant's down payment. It's only fair, therefore, that the tenant should also give up something in return for that concession. These kind of agreements can take many forms, and depend much on both market conditions and the negotiating skills of the parties involved. Legal advice is recommended.

There are also other tax implications. Under IRS residential replacement rules at the time of this publication, homeowners have two years before or after the sale to "rollover" profits into a replacement residence of equal or greater value. Thus, if you were to lease out your current home today and buy a new home of equal or greater value today, you could wait up to two years to sell the leased house without tax implications. After two years, however, you would owe the IRS tax on any "profit" on the sale of your former house. (The profit is the selling price less selling costs, improvement and original costs.) Keep that in mind in setting the lease length if you are considering a lease option or an alternative. There is also a potential tax liability due or the result of any depreciation taken on your present home if you rent it. The rules are complex and the advice of an accountant or tax attorney is suggested.

The following chapters are designed to help you get the best price for your home and reduce the time it takes to market the home. There are no foolproof formulas. What helps to sell one home might not help sell another. Mostly it's work and attention to details.

Best of luck.

SELLING YOUR HOME

CHAPTER I
SHOULD YOU SELL?

While there are many reasons why an owner or owners would want to sell their home, they do not always make good economic sense. The prospective seller should closely examine all factors to be sure the decision is a correct one. Some of the reasons for a decision to sell are:

1.) New job -- must move to another part of town/the state/the country
2.) Are ready for a nicer home with more space/ different rooms/better appointments.
3.) Decided I don't enjoy owning a home.
4.) Need cash to pay off debts/start business/pay medical bills.
5.) Sudden change of status/divorce, etc.
6.) Home is in a declining neighborhood.

Any one of these may be a good reason to sell. On the other hand, none of them would dictate that selling the home is the best idea in every case. What points argue against selling? If you've owned the home for some time, your monthly payments are probably low. You might also have a very favorable interest rate on an existing mortgage or you may be able to lower your monthly mortgage payments simply by refinancing.

You may also have considerable equity which could be borrowed against to meet financial needs unrelated to home ownership. Even if the reason for the sale is to enable you to buy a new home, it's entirely possible that you might be better off, from a tax standpoint, to keep the old home as an investment. An accountant knowledgeable of real estate tax law can work out the numbers for you relatively easily. While it's not always the best idea to own investment property in another town (in cases where you'll be moving out of town), perhaps you have family or reliable friends in the real estate management business who you would entrust to manage the property in your absence.

Perhaps remodeling or additions are the answer to a home not up to your rising standards. With transaction costs of selling one home and buying another often exceeding 10% of the selling price, some nice and substantial remodeling might be done with those savings. In some cases, a remodeler might be willing to offer financing, saving the effort and inconvenience of borrowing against your equity.

In many cases, thoughtful and prudent remodeling can increase the value of the home by as much or more than it costs. Among the types of projects that tend to add the most value, according to separate studies done for Kiplinger's Personal Finance Magazine and the National Association of Remodeling Industry, are kitchens, bathroom additions, and decks. Factors that affect the amount you will ultimately recover are whether the remodeling adds significantly to the utility of your home (adding a second bath to a one bath house will add more resale value than a fourth bath to a three bath house) or whether it "over improves" your home relative to others in the neighborhood.

Keep in mind that the right kind of remodeling can also help you sell your home faster, even if you do decide to move. Also keep in mind that the Better Business Bureau reports a high frequency of disputes between homeowners and remodelers and that many consumer organizations recommend that a formal written contract be used in major remodeling projects. The American Homeowners Foundation offers such a model contract. (See the "Other AHF Resources" section at the end of the book for more information.)

If you don't have, or can't spare cash for remodeling, there are other alternatives available. These include personal loans, home equity loans, and creative financing.

You can refinance your first mortgage and take out cash if you have sufficient equity in the home. This makes the most sense if your current mortgage rate exceeds rates available for refinancing and/or if you have a variable rate loan and would like to refinance to a fixed rate mortgage (or vice-versa). If your current mortgage rate is significantly higher than those available for refinancing you may be surprised to learn that you can take out cash and your monthly payments will increase little, if any. This approach also makes more sense if you plan to stay in the home a long time, since you are effectively spreading the cost of the remodeling as well as the up front loan costs (points, appraisal, settlement costs) over the term of the new mortgage.

If you don't anticipate being in the home for a long time, consider other financing methods or mortgage refinancing packages that do not require points or impose closing costs. The rate will be a little higher but you'll avoid the upfront costs.

If you're not going to stay in the home for a long time, or are remodeling to improve its salability, consider a home equity loan. This is a loan secured by the equity in your home (the fair market value less the balance of the first mortgage).

In most cases, the rate will be a little higher, in part because the security for the loan is subordinate to, or paid off only after the first mortgage in cases of default. On the other hand, many lenders offer home improvement loans without upfront costs. Most of the loans are not at fixed rates. Many float monthly based on economic indicators such as the prime rate, and not all have caps on the maximum rate over the life of the loan. Homeowners should be aware of the loan terms and wary of using such loans for financing over longer periods.

If you're borrowing under $17,500 see if any local lenders are offering FHA Title I home improvement loans, which have terms of six months to 15 years and do not require a lien on your home.

Another type of loan based on the equity in your home is a second mortgage. They are commonly for 5-15 years, and the rates are normally fixed. Closing costs are normally charged and the rates are normally higher than fixed rate mortgages. While the latter points might not seem to make them attractive, they do offer advantages under certain circumstances. If the rate of interest on your first mortgage is low it may not make sense to replace that loan, particularly since some of the upfront costs (the points) are in proportion to the amount financed. A second mortgage offers the security of a fixed rate, a certain advantage in uncertain times. In that regard, they minimize the risks of escalating monthly payments that are inherent in variable rate loans of longer term (10-15 years).

Another alternative is a personal loan -- i.e. a loan not secured by the equity in your home. These loans are generally of shorter duration and at higher rates. While tax laws enacted in 1986 allow for interest deductions on loans against home equity used for home improvements, they do not allow deductions for personal loans or credit card interest. Even though they loan is to be used for remodeling there arises a question both of documentation and the apparent contradiction in the tax law if a personal loan is to be used for this purpose. Given the other available alternatives there seems little reason for most to consider this alternative.

A final financing category is "creative" financing. Perhaps a remodeler may be willing to lend you part of the remodeling costs at a reasonable rate. Not all may be in a financial position to make such a loan and most will understandably want to record the loan on your house with the local government. The latter is standard practice among most home equity lenders. While remodelers may prefer higher rates and shorter terms, this is entirely negotiable. As individuals or small businessmen, they probably command no higher rates on their own savings than you -- anything above that rate is, in effect, a bonus for them. For the same reason your relatives might also be a source for such a loan.

A logical way to proceed would be to compare the packages from a number of available sources. Commercial lenders can provide you monthly payment and term information, total actual or estimated interest over the life of the loan, etc. If you are negotiating a loan with a remodeler or a relative, the loan tables in the back of this book can be used for those calculations.

Even if you must move for one reason or another, it does not necessarily follow that the only option you have is to sell your present home. It could be a wise idea to turn your home into a rental property.

There are some potential advantages and some disadvantages to this alternative. First of all owner occupants may sell their home and pay no taxes on the profits -- so long as the replacement residence was purchased within 24 months before or after the sale of your home. If you decide to rent out your current home, and you wait longer than 24 months after you purchase a replacement to sell the current residence, you would be taxed on the profits. That's a major disincentive for many people, except those who expect to realize no profit or are being temporarily transferred and expect to return to their present home within two years. For them it may indeed make sense to hold onto their current home and rent at the new location.

It might also make sense to rent out your current residence if you believe that the real estate market is at the bottom of a trough. If you expect substantial improvements in home values in the next year or two, a temporary rental may be a wise idea. If it appears to make sense, consider a lease with an option to buy. Under such an arrangement, a tenant usually pays a more than the going rental rate. Conversely, a significant part of the rent is subsequently credited towards a downpayment if the tenant subsequently decides to purchase the home.

This arrangement can be a win-win for both parties. The tenant, at the end of the lease, gets money credited toward a home purchase that would otherwise be gone for good. The owner gets a bonus if the option isn't exercised. The amount credited usually comes out to less than the typical 6% brokers commission. Lease option arrangements may set a specific price for the home or determine a procedure for establishing a fair market value. The latter is generally more in the seller's interest since the buyer is more likely to walk away if a predetermined price is over the subsequent fair market value. Conversely, you may regret the price you quoted if values rise substantially in the interim. You should hire a good real estate attorney to draw up a real estate lease purchase option or review the terms of any that you prepare.

While renting your home also offers other advantages -- your interest payments remain deductible and you can take a depreciation deduction for the house (but not the land), there are pitfalls as well. Renting is a headache -- it takes time to show the home and time and skill to select qualified tenants. The landlord is generally responsible for most of the repairs and even tenants with excellent credentials can turn out to be very irresponsible. Trying to act as an absentee landlord -- as when you live in a distant community -- only compounds the problem. While some real estate brokers offer rental management services, the fees are often expensive (10-15% of each month's rent). For that amount you'll get a monthly accounting of the status, but generally limited additional support. Plan on paying top dollar to mechanics they call in to make repairs at tenant request and expect a less than aggressive collection effort for overdue accounts.

Another argument against selling are the costs involved. Typically a real estate broker will get a commission of 6% of the total sale price, which will work out to a much higher percentage of your equity unless the home is paid for. On top of this there are costs associated with putting the home in "show" condition, not to mention closing costs, including "points" which can cost still more. If you could find a reason to wait a few more years, those costs will take a smaller bite out of an equity made larger by rising home prices and a declining loan balance.

There can also be problems for the owner of a home purchased recently. It's possible that there is no equity in the home once selling costs are taken into account. Indeed, with falling real estate values, some homes are now worth less than their purchase price.

Many times the decision to sell is based on some assumptions about the proceeds to be realized from the sale. The following worksheet should help you determine what you can expect to

HOW TO SELL YOUR HOME FAST

yield from the sale. A real estate broker can give you the prices of recent sales of similar homes in your neighborhood.

WORKSHEET I: Determining the Proceeds From the Sale of Your Home

	Optimistic	Pessimistic
1. Selling Price	_____	_____
2. Total Mortgage Balance(s)	_____	_____
3. Equity (Line 1 minus line 2)	_____	_____

Selling Costs

4. Fix Up/Clean Up Costs	_____	_____
5. Advertising Costs (selling yourself) or Broker's Commission	_____	_____
6. Attorney's Fees	_____	_____
7. Your Share of Real Estate Taxes	_____	_____
8. Real Estate Fees/Transfer Fees	_____	_____
9. Income Tax on Profits (0 if reinvested in home of same value or more within 2 years)	_____	_____

HOW TO SELL YOUR HOME FAST

10. Remaining Special _____ _____
    Assessments/Unpaid Liens

11. Minimum/Maximum Cost of _____ _____
    for Conventional/FHA/VA Loans

12. Other Seller Settlement Costs _____ _____
    or Purchase Incentives

13. Total Selling Costs _____ _____
    (Add Lines 4 to 12)

14. Proceeds (Subtract Line 13 _____ _____
    from Line 3)

CHAPTER II
SHINING THE APPLE

No smart seller would advertise their car for sale without at least cleaning out the glove compartment, vacuuming the floor and seats, and washing (maybe even waxing) their car. Some go even further and touch up paint chips, or maybe even repaint the car if the paint is badly faded and the car is worth enough so that the seller feels likely to recoup the cost of the paint job.

The same holds true with selling your home. There are many things that you can do to "shine the apple." Many will be likely to repay you handsomely for your time and/or expense. And of course there are some expenditures (of time or money) that are unlikely to return what you put into them. They may, however, make the difference between selling and not selling your home.

Even if you are short of both time and money, you may be well advised to undertake the most cost effective of these projects for several reasons. The first is that the return in terms of increasing the likely sale price is significantly greater than the time or money spent. The second is psychological. A rundown home creates an impression in a prospective buyer's mind of a homeowner who doesn't care. They will be likely to conclude, perhaps incorrectly, that everything else relating to the home is in equally rundown condition, from the appliances to the structure itself. Not only would an offer reflect these concerns, but the more likely result would be that you will receive no offer at all!

Determining what to do will require some subjective decisions. For example, it could cost a significant amount to have the interior of your home repainted. If the paint is in terrible shape and you know how to paint and have enough time to do it, you can reduce that cost tremendously while greatly improving the salability (and likely the selling price) of your home. On the other hand, if it's been painted a neutral shade recently and shows little sign of wear, your time and money would probably be better invested in other improvement efforts.

The first thing you should do is clean out and clean up. Clean out and get rid of anything you don't want or don't need. Give unwanted items to charity (for the tax deduction), throw them away, or have the yard sale you would have to have before you moved anyway. Wash and/or wax the floors, vacuum the rugs (shampoo if necessary), wash dirty walls, clean the windows. Clean out all closets and make sure when you go to hang things back up that there is plenty of space between hangers to create the impression of openness.

Make minor repairs such as replacing washers on dripping faucets. Replace inexpensive items that look shabby such as shower curtains or door mats. Get some spray from the pet shop if your pet isn't fully housebroken or doesn't smell like rose petals. Clean the drapes and install higher wattage light bulbs in fixtures in rooms that don't have lots of windows. Rearrange room furniture if necessary and get rid of anything that will give a cluttered appearance to your home. While you're at it, take down any political or religious posters, bumper stickers, buttons, etc. Your prospective buyer might not have the same political or religious philosophy as you and it's bound to color the buyer's attitude. If you find out that he or she does have the same views you do, you can put some of the materials back out when they come back for a second look. Brighten up your home with such things as a colorful new tablecloth for your dining room table, cut flowers, or some potted plants.

If yours is a detached home or a townhome, make sure the walks and driveways are swept, the lawn is mowed, and the garage or carport (if you have one) is cleaned out. If your home is not well landscaped, consider adding some inexpensive shrubs from your local nursery.

None of these suggestions involve spending much money, but they do take time. If time is a problem, consider hiring a maid and/or several neighborhood teenagers at a reasonable rate to help you with the process.

Major repairs are another matter. Should you replace an aging but operable refrigerator or sell it as is? You have a responsibility to be honest with brokers, agents and/or prospective buyers and should respond honestly to any questions about defects. On one hand, that information could turn off one prospective buyer while causing little concern to another who happens to be a refrigerator repairman. One possibility, especially if there are more than one or two significant problems, is to offer to pay some part of the cost of the replacement. If a home could use $1,000 worth of painting and $1,000 worth of replacement appliances/rugs or whatever, an offer to split the total $2,000 in the form of a decorating credit could be attractive to a prospective buyer, especially if the buyer also has the capability of doing certain amounts of the required work.

Use the fix-up checklist on the following page to make sure you have considered everything that might require cleaning or replacement. If you are planning to sell through a broker or agent, it's wise to do this work before you ask them to prepare a market analysis. The market analysis will reflect some subjective opinion about the home condition and is more likely to be accurate if the agent preparing the analysis is viewing the home in the condition in which it will be sold.

HOW TO SELL YOUR HOME FAST

WORKSHEET II: The Fix-Up Checklist

INTERIOR

Kitchen

Appliances cleaned inside and out? _____

Exhaust fan cleaned? _____

Walls cleaned, degreased if necessary? _____

Floor cleaned and waxed? _____

Cupboards cleaned, shelf paper replaced if necessary? _____

All electrical items working? _____

Sink cleaned, drain unclogged? _____

Counter tops neat, clean, and clear? _____

Windows washed? _____

Other? _____

Dining Room/Living Room/Den/Family Room

	Room 1	Room 2	Room 3
Paint or wallpaper cleaned/repainted/replaced?	_____	_____	_____
Carpet vacuumed/shampooed?	_____	_____	_____
Draperies/curtains cleaned?	_____	_____	_____
Windows washed?	_____	_____	_____
Furniture arranged for spacious appearance?	_____	_____	_____
Exposed wood dusted or polished?	_____	_____	_____
Lights operating, room brightly lit?	_____	_____	_____
Extra touches (flowers, etc.)?	_____	_____	_____
Closets cleaned?	_____	_____	_____
Other?	_____	_____	_____

Bedroom(s)

	Room 1	Room 2	Room 3	Room 4
Beds made?	___	___	___	___
Closets cleaned?	___	___	___	___
Paint/wallpaper cleaned/repainted/replaced?	___	___	___	___
Draperies/curtains cleaned?	___	___	___	___
Windows washed?	___	___	___	___
Furniture arranged for spacious appearance?	___	___	___	___
Exposed wood dusted or polished?	___	___	___	___
Lights operating, room <u>brightly</u> lit?	___	___	___	___
Extra touches (flowers, etc.)?	___	___	___	___
Other?	___	___	___	___

Bathroom(s)

	Room 1	Room 2	Room 3
Paint/wallpaper cleaned/repainted/replaced?	_____	_____	_____
Floors washed/tile recaulked/replaced?	_____	_____	_____
Joints caulked, grout cleaned?	_____	_____	_____
Sink, bathtub and/or shower cleaned, drains unclogged?	_____	_____	_____
Counter tops clean/clear?	_____	_____	_____
Faucets, shower heads, other fixtures cleaned, leaks repaired?	_____	_____	_____
Windows and mirrors cleaned?	_____	_____	_____
Fresh towels out, supplies stored, area disinfected,	_____	_____	_____

HOW TO SELL YOUR HOME FAST 31

new soap dishes?

Medicine cabinet
cleaned out _____ _____ _____

Other? _____ _____ _____

Halls

	Hall 1	Hall 2	Hall 3
Paint/wallpaper cleaned/ repainted, replaced?	_____	_____	_____
Carpet vacuumed/ shampooed, floors waxed?	_____	_____	_____
Draperies/curtains cleaned?	_____	_____	_____
Windows and mirrors cleaned?	_____	_____	_____
Exposed wood dusted/ polished?	_____	_____	_____
Lights working, halls brightly lit?	_____	_____	_____
Other?	_____	_____	_____

Fireplace

	Fireplace 1	Fireplace 2
Ashes cleaned out?	_____	_____
Wood/kindling neatly stacked on fireplace grate and/or in log holders?	_____	_____
Fireplace tools upright and cleaned?	_____	_____
Mantle and hearth cleaned?	_____	_____
Fireplace screen cleaned?	_____	_____
Other?	_____	_____

Basement

Storage items neatly packed? _____

Walls cleaned/repainted? _____

Dampness problems reduced or eliminated? _____

Floors swept/vacuumed? _____

Central heating/air conditioning

system cleaned? _____

Windows washed? _____

Lights operating, room <u>brightly</u> lit? _____

Other? _____

<u>Attic</u>

Storage items neatly packed? _____

Walls cleaned/repainted? _____

Floors swept/vacuumed? _____

Windows washed? _____

Lights operating, attic <u>brightly</u> lit? _____

Other? _____

<u>Plumbing</u>

Drips or leaks repaired? _____

All drains open? _____

<u>Electrical</u>

All circuits or fuses labeled? _____

All broken switches/switchplates/outlets replaced? _____

All exposed wiring properly sheathed? _____

<u>Heating and Cooling</u>

Filter replaced? _____

Annual/biannual servicing done? _____

Equipment accessible for examination? _____

<u>EXTERIOR</u>
(for detached homes and townhomes)

Lawn weeded, mowed, raked? _____

Shrubs trimmed/new shrubs added? _____

Driveways, walks, patios swept, weeds removed? _____

Fences, mailbox upright, repaired or painted if necessary? _____

Garage swept, tools/equipment/bicycles/etc. neatly stored? _____

Lights in garage/porch/front of home work? _____

Shutters straight/repaired/repainted if necessary? _____

HOW TO SELL YOUR HOME FAST

Home, garage, porch repainted if necessary? _____

Gutters straight, cleared? _____

Missing shingles replaced? _____

Exterior brass and chrome polished? _____

Doors and windows open smoothly? _____

Exterior windows cleaned, cracked panes replaced? _____

Antenna upright and in working order? _____

Other (list):

1. _____   8. _____
2. _____   9. _____
3. _____   10. _____
4. _____   11. _____
5. _____   12. _____
6. _____   13. _____
7. _____   14. _____

CHAPTER III

SETTING THE PRICE

There are two prices you must determine. One is the asking price and the other is the minimum selling price you will accept. Both are subjective decisions but should be made rationally based on facts. When home prices are relatively stable, it is fairly easy to determine the fair market value of most homes within several thousand dollars. However, one seller might need to sell in a hurry and be willing to accept something less than the "fair market value" for a quick sale. Another seller might feel, despite an objective appraisal, that the home is worth more for a variety of reasons and might, therefore, insist on a slightly higher price.

Setting the asking price requires the balancing of several opposing considerations. Setting a higher price certainly provides more room for negotiation, as well as the potential for an unexpected bonus should a buyer be willing to pay more than your minimum selling price. Realistically, however, you should recognize that the chances of the latter are relatively slim -- buyers are generally reasonably intelligent and reasonably well informed about the value of homes in a specific area. Also, setting too high a price has several potential risks. By discouraging informed buyers you may not get many (or any) offers, especially if you're in a buyer's market. The result may be a home that sits on the market for many months, which will discourage offers even further, not to mention the inconvenience and expense you will suffer as a result.

Determining the home's fair market value in a rapidly changing market, the first step before setting the price, is much more difficult. It's psychologically stressful in a declining market because it invariably requires rethinking expectations. There are fewer usable prior sales to use to gauge the value of your home. Not only are total sales usually fewer in a declining market, but sales that are more than a couple of months old may no longer accurately reflect the current market. As a result, it is much more difficult to get a true picture of the home's market value.

YOUR MINIMUM PRICE

The first step is to set the minimum price you will accept. It's important to do this for several reasons. The first is that it's better for your own mental health to set this price beforehand in order that you have a point of reference which you are confident in. If you don't do it, you may agonize over offers and find it extremely difficult to reach a decision as to whether or not to accept the offer or what kind of counter offer to make. You can easily lose a sale because of this hesitation. Secondly, this same point of reference will aid your negotiating strategy because you will know where you need to have the buyer end up.

There are several methods which can be used to determine the fair market value:

1.) Many prospective sellers will ask a real estate agent. Agents will usually prepare a market analysis which will include actual sales prices of similar homes in the neighborhood and additional subjective analysis. However, a particular real estate agent may not be experienced enough to have developed the ability to provide a reliable appraisal, or, even if experienced, they may not be knowledgeable about the values in your particular neighborhood. Further, an agent might purposely suggest a selling price that is lower than the true value of your home or might do just the opposite. Suggesting a lower than fair value amount might occur in a situation where the agent is confident of getting the listing and realizes that it's much easier and quicker to sell an underpriced home. Indeed, in a declining market one of the most effective ways of enhancing the likelihood of a sale is to price the home under the market. The commission is a few dollars less, but it's understandable why some agents would gladly accept a few dollars less when so many homes are not selling at all.

An agent might also suggest a higher than fair value selling price in a case where the agent believes the seller is considering other agents as well. (This is much more common in a stable or appreciating market.) It's easy to understand why a seller might be favorably disposed to an agent who suggests that the seller's home is worth quite a bit more than another agent's estimate. What happens, of course, is that after you select the agent suggesting the highest price, the home sits on the market for several months with little or no response. The agent then suggests a "market adjustment" or other euphemism which simply means "Let's lower the price to something closer to the true value." the net result is that you've wasted several months before the home is actually in a competitive position.

2.) If you are thinking about selling your home without an agent, you can visit your local courthouse and look up recent selling prices of similar homes in your neighborhood yourself. (Do not use "assessed" values. These are set by county personnel who have learned that it's much easier on relationships with the citizenry to undervalue the homes by 10% - 20% and make up the difference in tax rates, rather than deal with countless assessment complaints and appeals from taxpayers.) It is obvious that the homes used for comparison should be similar to your home in as many respects as possible -- size, age, construction, style, condition and most importantly, location. These days, the financing terms are an important consideration as well. A home sold with a low interest assumable existing mortgage, a low down payment, and/or a low interest second trust carried back by the seller would obviously be able to command a higher price than an identical home which required a new mortgage at current interest rates.

3.) The best (and most objective) means of determining the true value of your home is to hire a professional residential real estate appraiser. Most reliable appraisers belong either to the American Institute of Real Estate Appraisers and/or the Society of Real Estate Appraisers. The appraisal fee is based on the value of the house. They typically cost $150 and up and are a deductible selling expense. (You could also point out to the potential buyer that the appraisal you paid for is an expense the buyer might otherwise have to incur to qualify for a loan.) An appraisal should list the condition of all structural elements and systems. As a wise seller you should treat the appraiser as you would a prospective buyer -- pointing out upgrades (especially those not visible such as upgraded insulation in an older home -- new equipment purchases, etc.) Urge the appraiser to note such upgrades in the appraisal report.

A special note of caution should be considered by homeowners contemplating seller financing. You should, in any event, consult a real estate attorney to insure that any loans you extend are properly secured, legally executed, enforceable, insurable, and saleable. In the event of a default, a first mortgage must first be paid. If you hold a second, you will be paid whatever may be left over after the cost of foreclosure, the payment of the first trust, and the costs associated with the disposal of the property, which may often be at a distressed price. If the down payment is less than 10%, a combination of neglect on the part of the new owner, a depressed market, and the costs associated with foreclosure could leave you with less than the amount you're owed. To account for the added risk factor, second trusts of this sort will generally (and reasonably) carry an interest rate in inverse proportion to the down payment as a percent of the selling price. If a buyer is willing to put 20% or more in cash down, you are generally pretty well secured against risks and might reasonably offer a lower interest rate on the portion financed. If the buyer can or will only put 10% (or even 5%) down and expects you to hold a second trust, you should demand a higher interest rate to account for the risk of potential loss.

A second trust carried back by the seller can make sense for both buyers and sellers. The buyers usually end up with a package more favorable than a commercial loan. Since second trusts usually carry a higher interest rate than first trusts, the income generated by the trust will often be more than the financing costs on the same amount of money through a first trust. This means if the seller had been considering using all or part of the proceeds as part of a substantial downpayment on a replacement home, taking back a second is usually a wash at worst from a cashflow standpoint. The downpayment on the next home is reduced by the amount taken back on the second trust, but the interest income from the second trust will usually match or exceed the additional costs from increasing your first trust on your next home by the same amount.

Second trusts have other disadvantages besides risk to the seller's principle. Second trusts are not very liquid. They can be sold to private investors, but those investors will "discount" the note to achieve a higher interest rate. (If the balance due on the 10% note is $10,000, they might offer only $5,000 for the note in order to increase their effective interest rate to 20%). Furthermore, if you are moving out of the area, it's harder to keep pressure on a slow-paying buyer and harder and more costly to initiate foreclosure action.

SETTING THE ASKING PRICE

Setting the asking price is a much less objective process. Nevertheless, there are several generalizations which are appropriate:

1.) Most people ask more than they expect to realize from the sale of their home. In a seller's market they tend to get closer to their asking price. In a buyer's market they need to be willing to take less unless they have the flexibility of waiting as long as necessary to sell it.

2.) The greater the flexibility of the seller, the more sense it makes to offer the home at a higher price. Some ask 10%, even 20% more than they will take to provide even more negotiating room. The positive side of this approach is that the flexibility gives you a greater chance of finding the buyer who considers your home the "ideal" and is willing to pay a little more than the "fair market value." The downside is that this buyer may not appear in the time you've allocated, however flexible, and you may waste countless hours maintaining and showing your home.

3.) The less the flexibility of the seller (i.e., a need to move to a new location quickly, personal problems, etc.) the more sense it makes to price the home close to or below the "fair market value." True, you may end up getting less from someone who might be willing to pay more, or you may be forced to sell the home at less than "fair market value," but your chances of selling the home quickly are greatly improved.

The bottom line is that there is no simple answer. "Flexibility" is a mental state. Everyone's psychological make-up is different. There is no easy answer. You must evaluate yourself and your needs and make decisions appropriate to your own circumstances.

CHAPTER IV

SELLING YOUR HOME: HOW TO GET A GOOD BROKER OR HOW TO MARKET IT YOURSELF

THE CHOICE

One of the most important decisions in the selling process is whether to use a real estate broker or whether to sell your home yourself. The statistics suggest that most people think using a broker is the best route -- over 75% of home sales are through brokers and, no doubt, a significant share of the remainder are transactions between relatives or friends. Virtually any real estate broker can recount numerous horror stories about misfortunes befalling inexperienced sellers who have attempted to sell their own homes.

On the other hand, many home sellers, and not just those who are professional real estate investors, feel just the opposite. Many of these individuals, even first time home sellers, believe that the services offered by a broker bear no relationship to the real value of the assistance provided. They feel that the total costs of marketing their home, including not only advertising, legal counsel, and accounting advice, but a fair value for their time invested in the selling process, is far less expensive than the

6% to 7% commission which otherwise would have gone to a broker. Moreover, many also contend that even the best real estate agent cannot be expected to provide the same level of quality in legal or accounting support, both of which are well advised whether or not you use a realtor. Most of these persons would agree that a reasonably intelligent, diligent individual who is willing to put forth the necessary amount of effort to learn how to market their home effectively can be as effective or more effective than a real estate agent and can net more money from the sale as well.

There are several adjectives in the last sentence which every prospective seller should consider carefully. You don't have to be a genius to sell your own home. Much of the sophisticated expertise required whether you sell yourself or use a broker is available from an accountant or a real estate attorney. Nevertheless, you must possess some degree of marketing instinct, some appreciation for the nuances of human personality, and enough common sense to recognize when it's time to seek available expert help. Another key consideration is time. It seems to work out for most of us that we either have time and little money or money and little time. If you don't have between 40 and 80 hours between now and when you want to put your home on the market to learn the major considerations of real estate transactions as well as how to market it effectively, and another 5-6 hours a week to actually market your home, you may well be better off using a real estate agent. Not only is time required, but motivation is also essential. Are you the type of person with great ideas but who usually has trouble with the follow through? If so, selling your own home may not be the route for you.

Nevertheless, there are real advantages to those individuals with the common sense, motivation, and time to sell their own home. It's not as hard as it may seem initially. When you consider that a 6% commission on a $70,000 home amounts to $4,200, and that the out-of-pocket advertising costs would probably be a fraction of that amount, then it's understandable why an extra $3,000-$4,000 profit could seem very tantalizing indeed.

Like so many other aspects of real estate, this too requires a subjective decision. If you have the luxury of time, you may want to try to sell your home yourself initially and then turn to an agent if your efforts are unsuccessful. Or you may want to do both simultaneously -- inserting a provision in your listing agreement that no commission is due if you sell your home yourself. Brokers generally dislike such provisions for obvious reasons, but few will turn down a listing for that reason alone.

Keep in mind that the ability of an individual to sell a home without the assistance of a broker and an agent is related to home supply and demand. In a seller's market, when the broker cannot get enough homes to sell, the idea makes much more sense. Hungry buyers will be looking diligently for any available homes, spending more time reading the want ads and driving through desired neighborhoods.

When there is a glut of sellers and a shortage of buyers, the opposite holds true. The fewer buyers will find many aggressive real estate agents with the time to seek them out and plenty of time to work with them. The multiple listing service provides a tremendous advantage to sellers using brokers and agents in such circumstances. It enables buyers to obtain information about more listings that meet their needs than the buyers probably have time to see. In such an environment a homeowner marketing his or her own home without an agent or broker will have a very difficult time attracting potential buyers even if they are doing a first class job of marketing the home.

A compromise is to use a "discount broker," who charges significantly less than the 6% rate charged by most brokers. Some charge a flat rate, others a commission only if the home sells, and others a combination of both. These brokers will put your home in the multiple listing service (the broadest possible exposure) or in a private listing service (much less exposure). They may provide limited additional assistance, such as providing for sale signs, buyer followup, advertising, and/or cooperative advertising opportunities, but they do not generally provide agents who will show your home and/or bring potential buyers. Discount brokers are a relatively new phenomenon and some have gone out of business. Since some up front fee is normally required, it's in your interest to look into their economic health before paying a fee if one is charged.

Still another option is to negotiate the commission rate with a "conventional" broker. While most conventional brokers and brokers do not mention it, the rate of commission is negotiable.

Under the right circumstances, some will charge less than the 6% or 7% typical of most listings. They would be most likely to negotiate if there is a current shortage of listings (i.e. a seller's market) and/or if the home is to be priced competitively, the homeowner offers to help in holding open houses, etc.

Another thing to keep in mind is that particular buyers often have close working relationships with real estate agents. These "buyer" agents technically owe their allegiance to the home seller. They are compensated by sharing the commission (typically the agent listing the home and the broker will split one half of the commission; the buyer's agent and his/her broker will split the other half). Since the buyer's agent works on commission, he or she will be reluctant to show a prospective buyer a home that either has a lower than average rate of commission or is offered for sale by owner with no commission.

It can therefore be to the private seller's advantage to offer a commission to a buyer's agent for bringing a buyer. It's a subjective decision as to whether the "normal" 3% buyer agent/broker commission is worth it. If you are willing to pay that commission, that information should appear on your promotional ads and brochures. It can be a false economy, when using a discount broker, to offer less than the going commission rate to the buyer agent/broker. In a slow market with few buyers, agents will be most reluctant to show a home which offers a substandard buyer's agent commission.

Mentioning a specific buyer agent commission when you're selling your home yourself can also offer some additional protection. Sometimes an agent might bring a prospective buyer to your home during an open house. Absent any written notice of a commission rate, courts in some states have held the homeowner liable for the full (normally 6%) commission even though no listing agreement was signed or terms discussed.

An even better idea for sell-it-yourselfers would be to develop your own open listing agreement (always limit the duration) and have agents who bring clients by sign it before they come into the house.

Option I: Selecting a Broker

The process of selecting a broker is one which will also require some investment of time and energy. The right broker is not necessarily someone whom you would like, or someone who might become your best friend, but the right broker should not be someone with whom you are uncomfortable or distrust.

The right broker or real estate agent has a reputation for integrity and a proven record of successful sales in your area. Drive around your neighborhood and note which brokers have "for sale" signs and the names of any agents that may appear on them. The right broker or agent should be able to provide references from several satisfied former home sellers in your neighborhood. Contact those sellers and ask them what they thought of the agents/brokers they listed with using

HOW TO SELL YOUR HOME FAST 51

Questionnaire 4-1. Remember that a broker and an agent are part of a team -- both should have good credentials. If either is weak, the seller could suffer. If the agent is good but does not have adequate administrative backup, technical support, and other support services which could be required from the broker, the seller could suffer. Your local Better Business Bureau is another source of information.

When you meet with a prospective agent or broker, formally interview them. *You* are the client and *you* have the freedom of choice to select which representative you will allow to profit from your selection. Use a questionnaire like example 4-2 and interview at least two or three likely prospects. They may have to get back to you with some of the information, and their response time is also a good indication of their interest in your business.

QUESTIONNAIRE 4-1

BROKER REFERENCE FORM
(for customers of agents and brokers you are considering)

1.) Name of seller_____
   Address_____
   _____
   _____
   Telephone_____
2.) Name of selling broker and agent
   _____
   _____

3.) On a scale of 1 - 10 (10 being best), how would you rate the:
   a. agent   1 2 3 4 5 6 7 8 9 10
   b. broker   1 2 3 4 5 6 7 8 9 10
4.) What was the asking price of the home
   _____

5.) What was the selling price of the home
   _____

6.) How long was the home on the market
   _____

7.) a. Was the home sold by your original listing broker?
   _____ yes   _____ no
   b. If no, which agents/brokers were unsuccessful?

_____

_____

_____

8.) If you were selling the same home again, would you use the same agent and broker? _____ yes _____ no

9.) Any other suggestions regarding agents or brokers in this market?

_____
_____
_____
_____
_____

QUESTIONNAIRE 4-2

BROKER/AGENT INTERVIEW

1.) Name of prospective agent
   _____
   Company
   _____
   Business address
   _____
   Home phone_____
   Work phone_____
2.) Age of brokerage company _____
   number of offices _____
   total number of employees _____
3.) Agent's total experience _____ years;
   full time _____ part time _____
4.) Number of homes listed in last 3 years:
   last year_____ year before_____ 3 years ago_____
5.) Number of homes sold in last 3 years:
   last year_____ year before_____ 3 years ago_____
6.) Number of homes listed in last 3 years in your neighborhood (you must define boundaries of market for the agent):
   last year_____ year before_____ 3 years ago_____
7.) Number of homes sold in your market in last 3 years:

HOW TO SELL YOUR HOME FAST 55

by the prospective agent - yr 1 ___ yr 2 ___ yr 3 ___
by others in his/her firm - yr 1 ___ yr 2 ___ yr 3 ___
8.) What kind of marketing program does the agent envision for your home? What publications will it be marketed in?
a. _____ b. _____ c. _____

How frequently?
a. _____ b. _____ c. _____
9.) Date of interview _____
10.) Date agent provided additional information _____

TYPES OF LISTINGS

There are several listing options for sellers deciding to use the services of a broker.

A. <u>Exclusive Right to Sell</u>. This is perhaps the most frequent method. The listing broker is entitled to a commission no matter who sells the property, even if it is the homeowner. The broker can share that commission with another broker who produces a buyer under a cooperative arrangement, but you will be charged only one commission at the agreed upon rate. This method is preferred by most brokers and generally results in the most marketing support. On the other hand, you have to pay the commission even if a friend, neighbor, or colleague learns of the sale from you and is willing not to use a broker. If you know an individual who is interested in buying your home some brokers may be willing to add language to the listing agreement exempting you from an obligation to pay a commission if that named individual does purchase the home.

B. <u>Exclusive</u>. An exclusive listing is the same as the exclusive right to sell except that you may sell the property yourself without paying the commission. A broker will be less interested in this type of listing unless you have a specific client in mind. Agents and brokers are taking a risk (justified in some cases) that the seller will choose to negotiate directly with a prospective buyer solicited by the broker after the listing expires, thus depriving them of a legitimate commission. If you, as a seller, encourage such an action, you would not only be acting unethically, but could be subject to a lawsuit for the commission.

C. Open. An open listing is one which allows you to list with several brokers and requires you to pay the commission only to the broker who finds the buyer for your property. As you might suspect, brokers are reluctant to accept open listings, and when they do, can be expected to spend relatively little money or effort marketing the property.

D. Net listing. A net listing specifies that the commission you will owe the broker will be the difference between a specified amount -- "your net" -- and the amount the broker or agent can get for the home. This may or may not be a good idea depending on your circumstances. If a broker is willing to guarantee a "net" of the fair market value or close to it, it could be a good deal for the seller if the broker also agrees to provide satisfactory marketing backup. On the other hand, a wise broker would not likely agree to such a net listing unless the home was priced low enough that they believed they could sell it quickly and still yield the net after a normal commission.

Multiple listing services are common in most localities and are a means for dissemination of your home's availability for sale to other brokers whose agents may have prospective buyers who might be interested in your home. This service is normally available only when you deal through one broker.

PITFALLS AND OTHER CONSIDERATIONS

A wise seller protects himself or herself when selling through a broker. Normally you will be required to sign a listing agreement which is a contract specifying the rights and responsibilities of both parties. The forms are often standardized, but there is nothing to stop you from adding, deleting, or changing terms of the agreement. Some considerations you should take into account are:

A. <u>Length of listing</u>. Many broker will ask for a listing for three to six months, or even one year. (At the conclusion, the contract expires and you are again a "free agent.") You should consider a shorter term, perhaps one to three months, especially if your home is being advertised at close to the "fair market value." This gives the agent and broker more incentive to find a buyer promptly. An aggressive marketing plan, set out in writing as an addendum to the listing contract, specifying how your property will be marketed and in what advertising mediums as well as the frequency of open houses may justify a longer listing period. This will also provide backup documentation should you wish to cancel the agreement prior to the expiration date due to lack of "good faith effort" to find you a buyer.

B. <u>Automatic continuation of a listing agreement</u>. Never agree to an automatic continuation of a listing agreement (these are often in fine print). If you feel the service has been good, there is nothing wrong with signing a new listing agreement.

You should also consider adding any new marketing requirements or other conditions which are suggested by your experience during the first listing.

C. <u>The commission</u>. The commission is negotiable but most brokers will ask for 6% to 7%. There may be special circumstances where you may wish to offer less commission (for example, you are asking a very low price and/or would be willing to contribute in various ways to the marketing effort). Commissions are normally deducted from the proceeds at closing, but you may wish to suggest other arrangements. These should be included in the listing agreement and sales contract.

D. <u>The listing agreement</u>. The listing agreement should cover all property and appurtenances included in the selling price and all excluded from the sale. The listing should include relevant information on the proximity of schools, churches, fire and police departments, etc. You should receive a copy of the listing agreement.

Option II: Selling it Yourself

You've gone through the exercise of deciding whether to sell, you've either "polished the apple" or you are getting ready to, and you've set the price. After considering the pros and cons of using a broker you've decided to sell the home yourself, (or signed a listing agreement which excludes any obligation to pay a commission on a sale by owner). What's next?

THE MARKET PLAN

The next step is to develop a formal written market plan to reach prospective buyers for your property. You won't have some of the advantages of the "volume" advertisers (the real estate brokers), but you will have some advantages unique to the owner.

First, find out which advertising mediums are used to market the bulk of homes in your area. Which of the major newspapers in your area carry the greatest number of ads for homes in your neighborhood, and on which days? What are the breaks for multiple insertions, i.e., 3 days in a row, 7 days in a row, and for each of these options for multiple commitments (i.e., the same ad for Friday - Sunday repeated on 6 successive or alternating weekends will usually be cheaper than the same ad on a one-time basis). If you sell sooner than expected, your normal loss is only that you will have to pay a rate closer to the 3 day one-time rate.

Check the same information for communication vehicles with smaller distributions. Consider community publications; civic association newsletters; "want ad" type publications; church, fraternal, or professional publications; etc. Don't forget the "freebies." How about free bulletin boards at your office or church, your local grocery or other stores in your neighborhood. Don't forget the "for sale by owner" sign in front of your home and maybe a couple of extras for nearby busy intersections.

HOW TO SELL YOUR HOME FAST 61

(Check into local ordinances before putting up any signs other than on your own property). Word of mouth is also a free means of communication -- tell your neighbors, your colleagues, your mailman and paperboy, and your friends. While only a real estate broker can legally receive a commission on the sale of a home, there is nothing illegal in giving a small "present" after the fact to a friend who has referred a buyer.

Use the following worksheet to help you develop a market plan/budget for the sale of your home. Allow for a realistic selling period, at least as long as the current average for homes on your local multiple listing service. After you've added up the total costs, consider eliminating those expenditures that may not be cost effective and/or reduce the size or frequency of paid ads if the total budget is more than you can afford.

WORKSHEET 4-3: Market Plans

1.) Commercial publications

	Cost of Ads[1]	Number Placed	Total Cost
Newspaper A			
Newspaper B			
Newspaper C			
Other (specify)			
Community Publication			
Civic Association Newsletter			
Church, Fraternal, Professional Newsletter			

2.) Freebies

	Number Placed
Grocery Store A	
Grocery Store B	

HOW TO SELL YOUR HOME FAST

Grocery Store C   _____

Office Bulletin Board   _____

Point of Purchase (your home)   _____

Other Retail Outlets   _____

TOTAL --   _____

[1]Based on the number of ads times the price per line.

A key component of a marketing effort is a good brochure. Two brochures, one for bulletin boards and one to hand out to visitors to your home is even better. The one for bulletin boards should have tear off phone numbers along the bottom for convenience.

A good brochure should contain all the information listed on a standard multiple listing form and more. A good format is 8-1/2 X 11 inches. For handouts to prospective buyers who visit your home use the back of the brochure for more promotional prose, photographs of the house and/or rooms which show it to its best advantage, floor plans and/or other information which you want to remind buyers about when they review their materials later. Remember that buyers may look at dozens of homes over a short time span and will have trouble linking the typical undecipherable multiple listing form to a specific home. Your goal is to aid them in that effort and at the same time remind them of key features they should like about your home.

The quality of offset printing and photo copying has increased in recent years and prices have decreased. Standard black and white (and often even color) pictures reproduce much better. You should be able to get about 500 copies of an 8-1/2' X 11" brochure printed on two sides for around $25. Photographs are also inexpensive and you should be able to obtain 4 to 5 good photographs out of a roll of 24 (or 36) frame 35mm film. Film processing and printing should run around $10.

A standard format example is shown in Worksheet 4-4, on the following page. Style refers to general categories (i.e. rambler, colonial, split level, etc.) Construction is normally frame or brick. Siding types include vinyl, aluminum, wood, etc. Energy sources are normally gas, electric, oil or propane. The floor where the kitchen, dining room, and living room are located is normally considered the main floor. The level below would be the lower floor, regardless of whether it's finished or an unfinished basement. (On a split level it's a half floor below the main level.)

You should fill in either yes or no in the spaces for carpeting, dishwasher, disposal, etc. Normally anything which is either built-in or integral to the function of the home is considered to be included in the selling price. Unless specifically excluded such items as the refrigerator, stove, cabinets, light fixtures, wall to wall carpeting are presumed to be included in the selling price. Not normally included are such things as blinds and drapes, furniture, rugs (except wall to wall). It is common for sellers to include such items as custom drapes or blinds in the selling price, and not unusual for sellers to want to keep some items which normally convey to the buyer. If there is any doubt as to the status of an item you want to either keep or sell with the house, list it in the appropriate category to be safe.

WORKSHEET 4-4: Sample Format for Marketing Brochure

HOME FOR SALE BY OWNER

Description:

_____
_____
_____
_____
_____
_____
_____

Address

_____

City _____ State _____ Zip _____
Owner(s) _____
Phone (Hm) _____
Phone (Wk) _____

Style/type _____   Purchase year _____
Construction _____   Condition _____
Lot size _____   Taxes (annual) _____
Age _____   Roof _____
Builder _____   Siding _____

Room Sizes: (dimensions appear in column indicating floor location)

Rooms/Floor	Lower	Main	2	3	4
Living	___	___	___	___	___
Dining	___	___	___	___	___
Kitchen	___	___	___	___	___
Bath(s)	___	___	___	___	___
Family Room	___	___	___	___	___
Den	___	___	___	___	___
Utility Room	___	___	___	___	___
Master Bdrm.	___	___	___	___	___
Bdrm. 2	___	___	___	___	___
Bdrm. 3	___	___	___	___	___
Bdrm. 4	___	___	___	___	___
Bdrm. 5	___	___	___	___	___

Additional features of this home:

_____carpeting   _____dishwasher

_____disposal   _____storms/screens

_____fireplace(s) (indicate number)

other: _____

_____
Energy sources:

    Heat _____

A/C _____

Stove _____

Hot Water _____

Other _____

Average Monthly Sewer cost (or septic) _____
Average Monthly Water cost (or well) _____

Schools/distance:
   Elementary _____/_____
   Jr. High _____/_____
   High _____/_____
   Parochial(s) _____/_____

Other items included in the price
_____
_____

Items excluded from the price
_____
_____
_____

Directions:_____
_____
_____

Mortgage:
 PITI:_____Balance_____Rate_____%
 Yrs remaining_____
 Type_____Assumable?_____

Other Remarks:
_____
_____
_____

CHAPTER V

NEGOTIATING

There is no better way to study the quirks, irrationalities, and idiosyncrasies of people (including yourself) than experiencing the process of buying and selling a home. As a seller, you want to maximize your proceeds (which is not always the same thing as maximizing the selling price) just as the buyer wishes to minimize the cost. You will likely experience all sorts and manners of potential buyers; some serious shoppers and some window shoppers, some willing to pay a fair price for the right home and some shrewd, tough negotiating investors who only buy at distressed prices, some naive and some sophisticated, some pleasant and some unpleasant, some rational and many totally irrational.

If you are selling your home yourself, you'll be spending much of your time getting to know the best and the worst of this lot. Even if you're using a real estate agent, their personality and other characteristics are important. You should try to learn about the individual characteristics of your potential buyer because they will influence your negotiating strategy.

Your "ace in the hole" is that you have already gone through a rational process of setting a reasonable (based on your circumstances) minimum selling price which you are comfortable with. It doesn't make any difference where the bidding starts.

That knowledge should give you a significant advantage in the negotiating process.

Many prospective buyers like to play a game called "wouldyatake." (Wouldyatake $3,000 less, wouldyatake a second trust, etc.). These are reasonable questions for a prospective buyer to ask, but the seller should beware. If you say "yes" to "wouldyatake $3,000 less," you haven't sold the home or established any other terms of the sale, you've only established that you'll take at least $3,000 less and you have invited the prospective buyer to try for an even lower figure. In addition, verbal offers are not legally binding. Therefore, the smartest response for a seller to a "wouldyatake" is either "no" if the suggestion is out of the question, or "I'll consider all reasonable written offers," which is a much better response than "yes."

It is not unusual for a serious prospect to want to visit your home three or four times before deciding to make an offer (or deciding that your home is not quite what they wanted after all).

A key part of the negotiating process occurs when the prospect visits your home. You should always maintain a pleasant cordial attitude. Respond positively to anything the prospect says. If the prospect likes your large master bedroom, say something like, "We enjoy it very much too, and the large closets are really an extra plus." If the prospect says something negative like, "Your home is very similar to the home for sale across the street, which is selling for $2,000 less," you might say, "The Jones' home is a very good value for that price, but this home has been freshly painted and has a fenced yard and much better landscaping." Always avoid arguing with prospects. If they think the kitchen is too small although it may be bigger than most, the prospect could be wrong, but could also be a gourmet cook who wants a very large kitchen. It's much better to respond with something like, "I've found the layout to be very easy to work with and it certainly has a tremendous amount of cabinet space."

Accompany the prospects on a tour through the home. Even the most careful prospects will miss some of the good features. Don't be shy about pointing out things they have missed: "Did you notice this lovely view from the living room window? The sunsets are also lovely."

At some point in time a prospective buyer will want to make an offer and you should always insist that it be in writing. The minimum information required for a valid offer is the identification of the property, the date, the amount offered, and the signature of the individual(s) making the offer. If the offer is adequate, you need only write "accepted by owner(s)," sign it and put the date after your signature(s).

While this minimal information is all that is legally required, most real estate contracts contain much more information. It is in the interest of buyer and seller that the terms of what has been agreed to be as comprehensive as possible.

There is no national standard for a real estate contract, because laws affecting the sale of real estate vary from one jurisdiction to another, and because opinions vary among real estate attorneys and brokers in any jurisdiction. Local brokers can provide samples of contracts used by their firms. Since you should use a real estate attorney when you settle you should ask the attorney to provide or develop a single contract for use by prospective buyers if you're not using a broker and agent (most brokers' contracts are copyrighted and are for use only by their clients.)

It is rare that you will get a "full price" offer (at least not without unacceptable contingencies) and not all that common to get an offer which meets your minimum requirements the first time around. Let's assume you are asking $75,000 for your home but are willing to accept $70,000. Your goal is to make sure that any counters end up with the difference being $70,000 or more. Here's two examples of how you might negotiate and get your minimum price or better:

<u>Case 1</u>

1. Buyer offers $65,000

<u>Case 2</u>

1. Buyer offers $60,000. (This buyer may not be serious, but might also be trying to find out how low you'll go -- you're willing to drop $5,000 from your asking price but you've got to get the buyer to go up at least $10,000 -- or a

2. Your counter offer should be $72,500, not the $70,000 you have established as your minimum. If you counter with $70,000 that the buyer will likely try to reduce it still further and may break off negotiations if you don't have some flexibility left. The buyer might take your first counter, but might just as easily . . .

$2 increase for every $1 you drop.)

2. You counter with either $75,000 or $74,000. The former figure tells the buyer that he/she is nowhere near negotiating range while the latter tells the buyer that there's a long way to go.

3. Counter your counter with $67,500, in which case you should . . .

4. Counter with your most recent figure ($72,500) or with $71,500.

5. At this point <u>most</u> logical buyers with accept your last offer or raise theirs to at least $70,000.

It is rare that an offer will be as simple as that. More often there will be contingencies which may vary from reasonable to ridiculous. It is also reasonable for you to make a counter offer with reasonable contingencies of your own.

For example, a prospective buyer might put in the phrase, "this offer is valid for three days and is contingent on buyer obtaining financing." These are reasonable contingencies. The prospective buyer is giving you three days to make your decision so you won't have too much time to shop his offer around with other prospects in the hope of getting a higher price. Assuming the offering price and other terms meet your requirements, this should not be a barrier to the sale.

Assuming that the buyer will likely qualify for a loan (and you should "prequalify" the buyer before signing the agreement using the form appearing later in this chapter), the second part of the contingency presents only one problem: there is nothing that places any requirement on the buyer to qualify promptly. Unless you insert your own contingency "buyer to obtain financing within 30 days" or "buyer to apply for financing within two weeks," you are asking for trouble.

One important aspect of the sales agreement is the earnest money, which is the amount to be tendered by the buyer at the time the agreement is signed to show that he or she is in earnest. You should explain that the money will be held in a trust account by your attorney or real estate broker if you are using one. The amount should be as much as possible, perhaps as much as 5% of the value of the home. This money will be applied towards the down payment at the time of settlement.

Don't accept a small earnest money deposit, such as $100. It isn't enough to cover your loss if the buyer backs out of the deal, nor is it enough to cover the costs of possible legal actions for "specific performance" to force the buyer to honor the agreement. A person might walk away from a $100 deposit for a variety of reasons ranging from finding a home they like better to a subsequent disagreement with a spouse, but not many will walk away from several thousand dollars. Some buyers may not have 5% of the selling price in cash on hand for the simple reason that they may be prudent investors whose funds are tied up in long term investments such as treasury notes, equity in their current home, etc. This is understandable and you can get around this problem by allowing them to give you as part of your earnest money deposit a note, properly secured by specifically identified assets. The note should be prepared by your attorney.

An offer can be much more complex as well. There may be contingencies which you should reject for obvious reasons, as well as others which will require the help of an accountant, an attorney, or others to fully evaluate. Suppose for example, you have an assumable mortgage and the buyer wants to pay so much down and wants you to hold a second trust for a certain period of time at a certain rate. The price is at or above your minimum but you need all the equity for other purposes. In the case of such an offer you will have to find how much you can get for the second by selling it, usually at a discount, to individuals or institutions dealing in this market. Similarly, the price offered could be over your minimum but contingent on the repainting of your home. If you don't have the time or inclination to paint it yourself, you'll need to find the cost of painting it from a contractor in order to find out whether you will "net" your minimum. Other contingencies could require an attorney's explanation because they are in "legalese." (Don't accept the buyer's definition of the "legalese.") Likewise, complex financial contingencies might require the advice of your accountant.

Hopefully, any time limitation in the offer will allow you enough time to evaluate these considerations. If the buyer's not willing to extend the length of the offer, then you should add a contingency of your own such as "subject to the approval of seller's _____" (attorney, accountant, etc.) or "subject to an estimate of $ _____ or less for the repainting of the home."

Certain settlement costs must be paid by the buyer, others by the seller, while still others are negotiable (both requirements and normal practices vary among localities). A good idea is to try to get the buyer to pay as many of the "negotiables" as possible through the proper language in your purchase agreement.

PREQUALIFYING THE BUYER

As soon as possible, you should prequalify the potential buyer. This will save you time in negotiating with a buyer who would not be able to qualify for financing anyway. It will also give you some idea of the buyer's flexibility in terms of meeting your asking and/or minimum price. Explain that you will be taking your home off the market and possibly missing a possible subsequent sale if the buyer cannot afford the home. Before you do that you want some reasonable assurance that the buyer will be able to afford your home. Negotiations can begin or continue after the prospective buyer provides you the information, but in the meantime you can quickly find out if you have a qualified prospect.

Use form 5-1 (which follows). You may determine that the prospective buyer could afford to finance more or less than the asking price of your home. If the amount is less, you should inform the prospective buyer of this fact and ask the buyer whether he/she has the cash or liquid assets to make up the difference and cover his/her settlement costs.

WORKSHEET 5-1: Confidential Buyer Financial Statement

Name of Buyer(s) _____
Home Phone(s)_____
Current Address
_____

Present Employer
_____

Job Title _____
Length of Employment _____
Business Address
_____

Annual Income _____
Total Debts _____
Monthly Payments: Loans _____
Automobile _____
Credit Cards _____ Other _____ Total
_____

Second Buyer's Present Employer
_____

Job Title _____
Length of Employment _____
Business Address
_____

Annual Income _____

Total Debts _____
Monthly Payments: Loans _____
Automobile _____
Credit Cards _____ Other _____ Total _____

Other Income (specify sources) _____
_____
_____

Total Annual Income _____
(salaries, commissions,
dividends and interest)

Total Annual Expenses _____
(subtract)

Net Annual Income
(not including rent or mortgage payments)_____

Total amount which can be
financed with this net
income* _____

Buyer(s) total cash/liquid
assets available for down
payment _____

Total price buyer can afford
(total liquid assets plus

maximum amount which can be financed)_____

* This figure varies with current interest rates, financing plan selected, and among lenders. A typical maximum ceiling on monthly housing costs is no more than 28% of monthly income and no more than 36% of monthly housing costs plus all personal debt, including auto and personal loans and credit cards. Consult lenders in your area.

CHAPTER VI

FINANCING

Few people have a really good understanding of real estate financing, especially in the volatile market of recent years. Not only is it a foreign language to most buyers and sellers, but many good real estate agents, who may be talented in other areas, are not necessarily all that well versed in it themselves. Sources of financing include commercial banks, mortgage companies, savings and loans, life insurance companies, the buyer's relatives, and you. The loans may be guaranteed or backed by various governmental authorities (VA or FHA, etc.) or may not be subject to government participation, in which case they are called "conventional." Buyers may assume the seller's existing mortgage in some cases and the balance (less the down payment) can be financed by you or by those active in the secondary market.

It is in your interest to help your buyer get financing and in some cases may be in your interest to provide financing. Properly executed seller financed obligations can be sold (usually at a discount) on the open market. This process is becoming widespread enough that you, through your accountant, a bank, a real estate broker, or other sources, can find out how much cash you can get for the note. It could be that the proceeds from the sale of the note combined with the down payment could provide you with the total cash you require from the sale. In any event, it's easy to find out how much more down payment is needed and/or how the terms of the seller financing must be changed to produce the additional cash you need. Depending your circumstances, your accountant might also recommend that you hold on to the note as a wise investment from your own standpoint. After all, if you don't need all the cash and the return on the loan is better than you could do with other forms of savings or investment, seller financing could be as good a deal for you as it might be for the buyer. Even if you were to plan to use the proceeds for a significant down payment on your next home, you may still want to hold onto the note. If the rate on the seller financing exceeds the rate you will pay on your new mortgage, you'll actually make a profit on the transaction. If there is no prepayment clause in your new mortgage and you are holding a "balloon" note, you can take the proceeds from the balloon and reduce your new mortgage balance by the amount of the balloon payment when the balloon becomes due.

Seller financing (sometimes called creative financing) is a complex issue which very often will require the advice of a competent accountant and a competent real estate attorney. It can often mean the difference between a sale and no sale, and can be a winner or a loser for the seller.

Many mortgages from traditional lenders (savings and loans, commercial banks, mortgage banks, etc.) are sold on the "secondary" mortgage market, although the buyer may fail to recognize this because the original lender or loan servicer may still collect the monthly payments. The secondary market should not be confused with secondary financing. It involves exchanges between loan holders of first mortgages. This might happen when a savings and loan in one part of the country is overburdened with mortgage loans and sells them to an underburdened lender in another area.

The government is a major player in the secondary market. The oldest of the federal agencies is "Fannie Mae" (FNMA, which stands for the Federal National Mortgage Association and dates back to 1938). In 1968, it was divided into the current FNMA, a stockholder owned corporation and "Ginnie Mae," the Government National Mortgage Association. Ginnie Mae buys FHA insured and VA guaranteed mortgages and Fannie Mae, an agency of the Department of Housing and Urban Development (HUD), buys both as well as conventional mortgages.

More recent in origin is "Freddie Mac," the Federal Home Loan Mortgage Corporation, created in 1970 and owned by the dozen Federal Home Loan Banks (these banks back-up the savings and loans and pools and sells them through Mortgage Participation Certificates (MPCs) and Guaranteed Mortgage Certificates (GMCs) with principal and interest payments guaranteed by Freddie Mac.

Adding to the complexity is the Federal Reserve Board, which controls the money supply. Its policies influence the cost of credit which is directly related to mortgage interest rates.

Another factor in financing are the "points," each of which is equivalent to one percent of the total loan. Home sellers should learn the current points charged at various mortgage rates regardless of whether the loan is federally backed or not. They should also learn local rules and practice which determine who may or must pay those points.

The home seller should check the existing mortgage to see whether it contains an alienation or due-on-sale clause. If so, you should contact your original lender to determine whether or not they have sold your mortgage through the secondary market in a manner that affects the possible assumption of the loan. (Some lenders will allow an assumption, usually for a fee and/or increase in the interest rate, of a due-on-sale mortgage while others will enforce the clause.) Find this out before you negotiate with a buyer.

The real estate market has undergone incredible changes in the last several years. Most sellers are familiar with the traditional "fixed rate mortgages," but unless you purchased your home after 1980, you may not be as familiar as you should be with other financing options. You should familiarize yourself with each of the following types of financing so that you can explain them intelligently to prospective buyers unfamiliar with what is on the market today.

TYPES OF FINANCING:

FIXED RATE MORTGAGES

Mortgages with a fixed rate and term are the traditional form of mortgage. The majority of more than $1 trillion worth of outstanding home mortgage debt is in this form.

The fixed rate mortgage has no surprises. The first payment is the same amount as the last, which usually occurs 30 years later. Some are also available for shorter terms -- 7, 15 or 20 years, for example. Most of the early payments are interest, most of the later payments are principal. Subsequent changes in market rates do not affect these mortgages. Since the mortgage payments remain constant while most people's income rises during their career, the buyer will generally find that this payment requires a smaller share of the buyer's total income as time progresses. This leaves the buyer with an increasing amount of disposable income in later years for other purposes, whether they be improvements in lifestyle or savings for retirement, a nicer home, and/or children's education.

While these are considerable advantages, both points and interest rates may be higher than some of the more flexible types of loans. Some fixed rate mortgages may be impractical to refinance should interest rates decline further due to prepayment penalties and other costs. Since buyers are paying a premium for the certainty of the loan, they generally make more sense the longer they intend to own the property. Most recent fixed rate mortgages are not assumable by subsequent buyers at the same rate because they carry due-on-sale clauses. Rules relating to prepayment penalties, other refinancing costs, and due-on-sale clauses should be investigated thoroughly in this and all other types of mortgages available today.

GRADUATED PAYMENT MORTGAGES

These are also considered to be fixed rate loans, but the monthly payments in the early years are less than they otherwise would be in a conventional fixed rate mortgage, while payments in later years are higher than they otherwise would have been in order to make up the difference. Payments are normally structured to rise gradually for five years or so and then remain constant for the remainder of the loan term. They may be a conventional, VA, or FHA mortgage.

Because initial payments are lower in earlier years, they may enable a buyer whose income is expected to rise through the years to afford a nicer home (or enable a buyer who otherwise could not qualify for a home to at least buy something in the local market).

On the other hand, the fact that the payments go up each year for a certain number of years means that the buyer will have less disposable income during each of those succeeding years than they would have had with a fixed constant rate loan. The interest they don't pay in the beginning increases the buyer's indebtedness. If they sell after only a few years, they could end up owing more than they initially borrowed. Given even a modest rate of appreciation at the time of sale, the buyer would probably be ahead of the game, but keep in mind that recent history proves that buyers cannot always count on appreciation over a short term.

ADJUSTABLE RATE MORTGAGES

Adjustable rate loans are loans whose interest rate varies based on a formula related to some measure of current interest rates accompanied by rules that determine how quickly or slowly the interest may rise or fall. There are many types of ARMs, as they are called, and they are all a trade off. The lender seeks to have the buyer assume some of the risks of an increasing interest rate and in turn agrees to share some of the benefits of a declining interest rate. Thus, in most cases, succeeding payments could be more, less, or both, than the first payment depending on the changes in the market. There are often caps on how fast payments can rise or fall, as well as caps on the maximum interest rate. Some can be converted to fixed rate loans at specific times during the loan's duration. While there has been some trend toward uniformity, terms vary widely and it is crucial that borrowers compare, study, and understand the terms.

TAX IMPLICATIONS

The tax implications of the sale of your primary residence are pretty straightforward. There is no tax due on the sale provided that you buy a replacement home of equal or greater value within 24 months of the sale of your home. The 24 months works in both directions -- you could buy the replacement home up to 24 months before you sell your current home.

Equal or greater value means that the price of the new home must meet or exceed the adjusted selling price of the old home. If it is less than the adjusted selling price, the difference is taxable.

There is a one-time exemption to this rule available to homeowners age 55 or older and who have lived in their home for at least three of the previous five years. This once in a lifetime exemption allows qualifying individuals or couples to exempt up to $125,000 in taxable profit from the sale of a home. It could most benefit individuals "moving down" to smaller and/or more modest quarters. Often retired individuals or couples wish to avoid the hassles of home ownership, and indeed the ownership tax incentives are less for individuals who will be living on a smaller income. All home sales must be reported to the IRS on form 2119.

If you are providing financing for the buyer, the picture is more complicated. Depending on how the sale is structured you may owe taxes on the amount financed, and you will owe tax on the interest income. A competent accountant or tax attorney should help you during the negotiations related to seller financing to assure you that your legal tax obligation is minimized.,

Some costs relating to the sale of your home are tax deductible. These include certain fix up costs, commissions, legal fees, transfer taxes, appraisal and title costs.

Many of these same costs may be deductible if you are purchasing a new home. In addition, if the purpose for the sale was to take or look for a new job at least 35 miles farther from your home than the old job, some house hunting and moving expenses may be deductible too. Some of the eligible costs include job hunting trips, moving, travel to the new home and temporary food and lodging. Contact the IRS for a brochure describing additional restrictions and items covered.

CHAPTER VII

THE CLOSING

The closing can be a relatively uncomplicated process or it can take several hours (or not come off at all if the proper steps haven't been taken). You have to keep an eye on everything from the signature on the sales contract to the actual closing. Escrow closings do not require the presence of the buyer or seller. Instead each signs an agreement which sets out who must pay what to whom by when. Upon completion, the escrow is closed. A face-to-face closing is often called a settlement.

See that all involved, including the lending agency and your title attorney, have copies of the sales agreement. The title examination should be ordered as soon as possible and your attorney should prepare the paperwork necessary to convey the property. A survey is usually required if a new loan is being originated. The buyer should be provided an estimate accurate to within a few dollars of the amount required at closing.

Ask the buyer to advise you when he or she has applied for a loan (if a new loan is required) and then contact the lender and ask them to inform you when the credit application has cleared.

You must find out who needs to be at the closing. Anyone whose name appears on the deed must sign it and in some jurisdictions so must a spouse even if the spouse's name does not appear. Sometimes when one party is unavailable on the day of settlement, they can provide the power of attorney to others to sign on their behalf.

Find out when you'll get your cash, especially if it's needed for another investment. Even if the buyer produces a certified check, most settlement attorneys do not disburse checks until all necessary documents have been recorded.

You will need to bring a copy of the sales contract to the closing, as well as documentation that any contingencies have been removed or satisfied. The title insurance or abstract company and attorney or closing officer should have all papers necessary to complete the transfer. These may include, depending on your location, the deed, certificate of title, survey and title insurance policy, correcting affidavits, quitclaim deeds, and papers showing that all liens or judgments have been removed or satisfied. The prorations should have been worked out on such things as property taxes, assumed loans, insurance premiums, utilities, etc. You should have receipts or canceled checks showing that you've paid all your utility bills. A note from you should indicate the mortgage balance and the date to which your interest has been paid.

Some buyers will want to move in before settlement for a variety of reasons, but it's risky to allow them to do so. Bedrooms that looked big suddenly become too small when filled with furniture. The new buyers get the opportunity to develop a dislike for the neighbors and vice versa. Sometimes "minor deficiencies" can turn into "major defects" in the eyes of buyers.

If you do agree to early occupancy, do so only with a thorough tightly drawn written pre-occupancy agreement approved by your attorney. Go through the prequalification procedures and allot more of the total payments to rent (versus down payment) in case the buyer fails to qualify. Do not allow physical changes in the home prior to settlement, and insert a clause that the buyer is accepting the home in an "as is" condition.

SETTLEMENT/ESCROW WORKSHEET

1. Property Address

_____

2. Selling Price   _____
3. Down Payment (including deposit)   _____
4. First Trust (subtract line 3
   from line 2)   _____
5. Second Trust (where applicable --
   subtract lines 3 and 4 from line 2)   _____

CHARGES RELATED TO YOUR LOAN:

6. Appraisal Fee (varies, often about
   0.1% of the selling price)   _____
7. Loan Placement, assumption, or
   refinancing fee (also called points --
   varies with loan and lender)   _____
8. Credit Report (around $20)   _____
9. Prepayment of Interest on New Loan _____
10. Homeowners Insurance Premium   _____
11. Mortgage Insurance Premium   _____
12. Mortgage Insurance Settlement Fee _____

OTHER CHARGES RELATING TO SETTLEMENT:

13. Title Insurance (required by lender) _____
14. Owners Title Insurance (optional)   _____
15. Attorney's Fees, including title   _____

examination (negotiable, typically
$200 - $400)
16. Recording Fees (including deed, firs   _____
    trust and second trust, if applicable
17. Tax Escrow, other city/county/state fees   _____
18. Survey   _____
19. Estimated Total Settlement Charges   _____

CHAPTER VIII

REAL ESTATE GLOSSARY

Buyers and sellers will find this glossary helpful in explaining words and terms used in real estate transactions. There are, however, some factors that may affect these definitions:

1.) Terms are defined as they are commonly understood in the mortgage and real estate industry. The same terms may have different meanings in another context.

2.) The definitions are intentionally general, non-technical and short. They do not encompass all possible meanings or nuances that a term may acquire in legal use.

3.) State laws, as well as custom and use in various states or regions of the country, affect the meanings of certain terms.

A

Abstract (of title) — A summary of the public records relating to the title to a particular piece of land. An attorney or title insurance company reviews an abstract of title to determine whether there are any title defects which must be cleared before a buyer can purchase clear, marketable, and insurable title.

Acceleration Clause — Condition in a mortgage that may require the balance of the loan to become due immediately, if regular mortgage payments are not made or for breach of other conditions of the mortgage.

Agreement of Sale — Known by various names, such as contract of purchase, purchase agreement, sales agreement, according to location or jurisdiction. A contract in which a seller agrees to sell and a buyer agrees to buy, under certain specific terms and conditions spelled out in writing and signed by both parties.

Amortization — A payment plan which enables the borrower to reduce his debt gradually through monthly payments of principal.

Appraisal	An expert judgment or estimate of the quality or value of real estate as of a given date.
Assumption of Mortgage	An obligation undertaken by the purchaser of property to be personally liable for payment of an existing mortgage. In an assumption, the purchaser is substituted for the original mortgagor in the mortgage instrument and the original mortgagor is released from further liability under the mortgage. Since the mortgagor is to be released from further liability in the assumption, the mortgagee's consent is usually required. |//
	The original mortgagor should always obtain a written release from further liability if he desires to be fully released under the assumption.
	Failure to obtain such a release renders the original mortgagor liable if the person assuming the mortgage fails to make the monthly payments.

An "Assumption of Mortgage" is often confused with "purchasing subject to a mortgage." When one purchases subject to a mortgage, the purchaser agrees to make the monthly mortgage payments on an existing mortgage, but the original mortgagor remains personally liable if the purchaser fails to make the monthly payments. Since the original mortgagor remains liable in the event of default, the mortgagee's consent is not required to a sale subject to a mortgage.

Both "Assumption of Mortgage" and "Purchasing Subject to a Mortgage" are used to finance the sale of property. They may also be used when a mortgagor is in financial difficulty and desires to sell the property to avoid foreclosure.

<u>B</u>   Binder or Offer to Purchase — A preliminary agreement, secured by the payment of earnest money, between a buyer and seller as an offer to purchase real estate. A binder secures the right to purchase real estate upon agreed

terms for a limited period of time. If the buyer changes his mind or is unable to purchase, the earnest money is forfeited unless the binder expressly provides that it is to be refunded.

Broker (See real estate broker)

Building Line or Setback Distances from the ends and/or sides of the lot beyond which construction may not extend. The building line may be established by a filed plat of subdivision, by restrictive covenants in deeds or leases, by building codes, or by zoning ordinances.

<u>C</u> Certificate of Title A certificate issued by a title company or a written opinion rendered by an attorney that the seller has good marketable and insurable title to the property which he is offering for sale. A certificate of title offers no protection against any hidden defects in the title which an examination of the records could not reveal. The issuer of a certificate of title is liable only for damages due to negligence. The

protection offered a homeowner under a certificate of title is not as great as that offered in a title insurance policy.

Closing costs
The numerous expenses which buyers and sellers normally incur to complete a transaction in the transfer of ownership of real estate. These costs are in addition to price of the property and are items prepaid at the closing day. This is a typical list:

<u>Buyer's Expenses</u>

Documentary Stamps on Notes
Recording Deed and Mortgage
Escrow Fees
Attorney's Fee
Title Insurance
Appraisal and Inspection
Survey Charge
Escrow Fees
Attorney's Fee

The agreement of sale negotiated previously between the buyer and the seller may state in writing who will pay each of the above costs.

Closing Day
The day on which the formalities of a real estate sale are concluded. The certificate of title, abstract, and deed are generally prepared for the closing by an attorney and this cost charged to the buyer. The buyer signs the mortgage, and closing costs are paid. The final closing merely confirms the original agreement reached in the agreement of sale.

Cloud (on title)
An outstanding claim or encumbrance which adversely affects the marketability of title.

Commission
Money paid to a real estate agent or broker by the seller as compensation for finding a buyer and completing the sale. Usually it is a percentage of the sale price -- 6-7% on homes, 10% on land.

Condemnation
The taking of private property for

public use by a government unit, against the will of the owner, but with payment of just compensation under the government's power of eminent domain. Condemnation may also be a determination by a governmental agency that a particular building is unsafe or unfit for use.

Condominium — Individual ownership of a dwelling unit and an individual interest in the common areas and facilities which serve the multi-unit project.

Contract of Purchase — (See agreement of sale)

Contractor — In the construction industry, a general contractor is one who contracts to erect buildings. There are also contractors for each phase of construction: heating, electrical, plumbing, air conditioning, masonry, carpentry, and others.

Conventional Mortgage — A mortgage loan not insured by HUD or guaranteed by the Veterans'

Administration or other federal agencies. It is subject to conditions established by the lending institution and state statutes. The mortgage rates may vary with different institutions and between states. (States have various interest limits.)

Cooperative Housing
An apartment building or a group of dwellings owned by a corporation, the stockholders of which are the residents of the dwellings. It is operated for their benefit by their elected board of directors. In a cooperative, the corporation or association owns title to the real estate. A resident purchases stock in the corporation which entitles him to occupy a unit in the building or property owned by the cooperative. While the resident does not own his unit, he has an absolute right to occupy his unit for as long as he owns the stock.

D Deed
A formal written instrument by which title to real property is transferred from one owner to another. The deed should contain an accurate description

of the property being conveyed, should be signed and witnessed according to the laws of the state where the property is located, and should be delivered to the purchaser at closing day. There are two parties to a deed: the grantor and the grantee. (See also deed of trust, general warranty deed, quitclaim deed, and special warranty deed.)

Deed of Trust Like a mortgage, a security instrument whereby real property is given as security for a debt. However, in a deed of trust there are three parties to the instrument: the borrower, the trustee, and the lender (or beneficiary). In such a transaction, the borrower transfers the legal title for the property to to the trustee who holds the property in trust as security for the payment of the debt to the lender or beneficiary. If the borrower pays the debt as agreed, the deed of trust becomes void. If, however, he defaults in the payment of the debt, the trustee may sell the property at a public sale, under the terms of the deed of trust.

In most jurisdictions where the deed of trust is in force, the borrower is subject to having his property sold without benefit of legal proceedings. A few states have begun in recent years to treat the deed of trust like a mortgage.

Default	Failure to make mortgage payments as agreed to in a commitment based on the terms and at the designated time set forth in the mortgage or deed of trust. It is the mortgagor's responsibility to remember the due date and send the payment prior to the due date, not after. Generally, thirty days after the due date if payment is not received, the mortgage is in default. In the event of default, the mortgage may give the lender the right to accelerate payments, take possession and receive rents, and start foreclosure. Defaults may also come about by the failure to observe other conditions in the mortgage or deed of trust.

Depreciation	Decline in value of a house due to wear and tear, adverse changes in the neighborhood, or any other reason.
Documentary Stamps	A state tax, in the form of stamps, required on deeds and mortgage when real estate title passes from one owner to another. The amount of stamps required varies with each state.
Down payment	The amount of money to be paid by the purchaser to the seller upon the signing of the agreement of sale. The agreement of sale will refer to the down payment amount and will acknowledge receipt of the down payment. Downpayment is the difference between the sales price and the amount financed. The down payment may not be refundable if the purchaser fails to buy the property without good cause. If the purchaser wants the down payment to be refundable, he should insert a clause in the agreement of sale specifying the conditions under which the deposit will be refunded, if the agreement does not already contain such clause. If the

seller cannot deliver good title, the agreement of sale usually requires the seller to return the down payment and to pay interest and expenses incurred by the purchaser.

E Earnest Money   The deposit money given to the seller or his agent by the potential buyer upon the signing of the agreement of sale to show that he is serious about buying the home. If the sale goes through, the earnest money is applied against the down payment. If the sale does not go through, the earnest money will be forfeited or lost unless the binder or offer to purchase expressly provides that it is refundable.

Easement Rights   A right-of-way granted to a government agency, person or company authorizing access to or over the owner's land. An electric company obtaining a right-of-way across private property is a common example.

Encroachment   An obstruction, building, or part of a building that intrudes beyond a legal boundary onto neighboring private or public land, or a building extending beyond the building line.

Encumbrance A legal right or interest in land that affects a good or clear title, and diminishes the land's value. It can take numerous forms, such as zoning ordinances, easement rights, claims, mortgages, liens, charges, a pending legal action, unpaid taxes, or restrictive covenants. An encumbrance does not legally prevent transfer of the property to another. A title search is all that is usually done to reveal the existence of such encumbrances, and it is up to the buyer to determine whether he wants to purchase with the encumbrance, or what can be done to remove it.

Equity The value of a homeowner's unencumbered interest in real estate. Equity is computed by subtracting from the property's fair market value the total of the unpaid mortgage balance and any outstanding liens or other debts against the property. A homeowner's equity increases as he pays off his mortgage. When the mortgage and all other debts against the property are paid in full, the homeowner has 100% equity in his property.

Escrow	Funds paid by one party to another (the escrow agent) to hold until the occurrence of a specified event, after which the funds are released to a designated individual. In FHA mortgage transactions, an escrow account usually refers to the funds a mortgagor pays the lender at the time of the periodic mortgage payments. The money is held in a trust fund, provided by the lender for the buyer. Such funds should be adequate to cover yearly anticipated expenditures for mortgage insurance premiums, taxes, hazard insurance premiums, and special assessments.

F Foreclosure	A legal term applied to any of the various methods of enforcing payment of the debt secured by a mortgage, or deed of trust, by taking and selling the mortgaged property, and depriving the mortgagor of possession.

<u>G</u> General Warranty Deed — A deed which conveys not only all the grantor's interests in and title to the property to the grantee, but also warrants that if the title is defective or has a "cloud" on it (such as mortgage claims, tax liens, title claims, judgments, or mechanic's liens against it), the grantee may hold the grantor liable.

Grantee — That party in the deed who is the buyer or recipient.

Grantor — That party in the deed who is the seller or giver.

<u>H</u> Hazard Insurance — Protects against damages caused to property by fire, windstorms, and other common hazards.

HUD — U.S. Department of Housing and Urban Development. The Office of Housing/Federal Housing Administration

HOW TO SELL YOUR HOME FAST 117

within HUD insures certain home mortgage loans made by lenders and sets minimum standards for such homes.

I Interest — A charge paid for borrowing money. (See mortgage note.)

L Lien — A claim by one person on the property of another as security for money owed. Such claims may include obligations not met or satisfied, judgments, unpaid taxes, materials, or labor. (See also special lien.)

M Marketable Title — A title that is free and clear of liens, clouds, or other title defects. A title which enables an owner to sell his property freely to others and which others will accept without objection.

Mortgage — A lien or claim against real property given by the buyer to the lender as security for money borrowed. Under government-insured or loan-guarantee provisions, the payments may include escrow amounts covering taxes, hazard insurance, water charges, and special assessments. Mortgages generally run from 10 to 30 years, during which time the loan is to be paid off.

Mortgage Commitment — A witten notice from the bank or other lending institution saying it will advance mortgage funds in a specified amount to enable a buyer to purchase a home.

Mortgage Insurance Premium — The payment made by a borrower to the lender to protect lenders against loss in insured mortgage transactions. In FHA insured mortgages this represents an annual rate of one-half of one percent paid by the mortgagor on a monthly basis.

Mortgage Note — A written agreement to repay a loan. The agreement is secured by a mortgage, serves as proof of an indebtedness, and states the manner in which it shall be paid. The note states the actual amount of the debt that the mortgage secures and renders the mortgagor personally responsible for repayment.

	Mortgage (Open-End)	A mortgage with a provision that permits borrowing additional money in the future without refinancing the loan or paying additional financing charges. Open-end provisions often limit such borrowing to the original loan figure.
	Mortgagee	The lender in a mortgage agreement.
	Mortgagor	The borrower in a mortgage agreement.
P	Plat	A map or chart of a lot, subdivision, or community drawn by a surveyor showing boundary lines, buildings, improvements on the land, and easements.
	Points	Sometimes called "discount points." A point is one percent of the amount of the mortgage loan. For example, if a loan is for $25,000, one point is $250. Points charged by a lender can raise the yield on his loan. Buyers are prohibited from paying points on HUD or Veterans' Administration guaranteed loans (sellers can pay, however). On a conventional mortgage, points may be

paid by either buyer or seller or divided between them.

Prepayment   Payment of mortgage loan, or part of it, before due date. Mortgage agreements often restrict the right of prepayment either by limiting the amount that can be prepaid in any one year or charging a penalty for prepayment. The Federal Housing Administration does not permit such restrictions in FHA insured mortgages.

Partial prepayments shorten the duration of the loan but do not affect monthly payments on fixed rate loans.

Principal   The basic element of the loan as distinguished from interest and the mortgage insurance premium. In other words, principal is the amount upon which interest is paid.

Purchase Agreement   See agreement of sale.

Q	Quitclaim Deed	A deed which transfers whatever interest the maker of the deed may have in the particular parcel of land. A quitclaim deed is often given to clear the title when the guarantor's interest in a property is questionable. By accepting such a deed, the buyer assumes all the risks. Such a deed makes no warranties as to the title, but simply transfers to the buyer whatever interest the grantor has. (See deed.)
R	Real Estate Broker	A middle man who sells real estate for a company, firm, or individual. The broker does not have title to the property, but generally represents the owner on a commission basis. Buyers may also hire brokers to negotiate on their behalf, and this practice is growing.
	Real Estate Agent	An individual who works for a real estate broker.
	Refinancing	The process where a mortgagor pays off one loan with the proceeds

	from another loan.
Restrictive Covenants	Private restrictions limiting the use of real estate. Restrictive covenants are created by deed and may "run with the land," binding all subsequent purchasers of the land, or may be "personal" and binding only between the original seller and buyer. The determination whether a covenant runs with the land or is personal is governed by the language of the covenant, the intent of the parties, and the law in the state where the land is situated. Restrictive covenants that run with the land are encumbrances and may affect the value and marketability of title. Restrictive covenants may limit the density of buildings per acre, regulate size, style or price range of buildings to be erected, or prevent particular businesses from operating in a given area.

<u>S</u>

Sales Agreement	See agreement of sale.

Special Assessments	A special tax imposed on property, individual lots, or all property in the immediate area, for road construction, sidewalks, sewers, street lights, etc.
Special Lien	A lien that binds a specified piece of property, unlike a general lien, which is levied against all one's assets. It creates a right to retain something of value belonging to another person as compensation for labor, material, or money expended in that person's behalf. In some localities it is called "particular" lien or "specific" lien. (See lien.)
Special Warranty Deed	A deed in which the grantor conveys title to the grantee and agrees to protect the grantee against title defects or claims asserted by those persons whose claim against the title arose during the period the grantor held title to the property. In a special warranty deed the grantor guarantees to the grantee that he has done nothing during the time he held

title to the property which has, or which might in the future, impair the grantee's title.

State Stamps — See documentary stamps.

Survey — A map or plat made by a licensed surveyor showing the results of measuring the land with its elevations, improvements, boundaries, and its relationship to surrounding tracts of land. A survey is often required by the lender to assure him that a building is actually sited on the land according to its legal description.

T

Tax — As applied to real estate, an enforced charge imposed on property, to be used to support the governing body.

Title — As generally used, the rights of ownership and possession of particular property. In real estate usage, title may refer to the instruments or documents by which a right of ownership is established (title documents), or it may refer to the ownership interest one has in the real estate.

Title Insurance
Protects lenders or homeowners against loss of their interest in property due to legal defects in title. Title insurance may be issued to either the mortgagor, as an "owners title policy," or to the mortgagee, as a "mortgagee's title policy." Insurance benefits will be paid only to he "named insured" in the title policy, so it is important that an owner purchase an "owner's title policy," if he desires the protection of title insurance.

Title Search or Examination
A check of the title records, generally at the local courthouse, to make sure the buyer is purchasing a home from the legal owner and there are no liens, overdue special assessments, or other claims or outstanding restrictive covenants filed in the record, which would adversely affect the marketability or value of title.

	Trustee	A party who is given legal responsibility to hold property in the best interest of or "for the benefit of" another. The trustee is one placed in a position of responsibility for another, a responsibility enforceable in a court of law. (See deed of trust.)
<u>Z</u>	Zoning Ordinances	The acts of an authorized local government establishing building codes, and setting forth regulations for property land usage.

THE AMERICAN HOMEOWNERS FOUNDATION PRESENTS CREATIVE SOLUTIONS FOR AMERICAN HOMEOWNERS AND PROSPECTIVE HOMEOWNERS

The largest share of net worth of most Americans is in the equity of their home. Buying, selling, investing, remodeling and building decisions have a major impact on the lifestyle and economic future of most Americans. With careful planning and thought, you can make the difference in your ability to find money for your children's education, your retirement, refinancing, and other things. Making wise decisions and careful investments are the key to creating this wealth.

The American Homeowners Foundation is dedicated to helping homeowners deal with the responsibilities and requirements of owning your own home. That's why we have put together this selection of books, model contracts, special studies and services. Each one is designed to protect, enhance and develop your real estate investment. And, help you understand the process better.

Whether you are a current homeowner or a prospective homeowner, all of these products are designed with your needs and concerns in mind. Just look at the selections we are offering to you through this special introductory offer.

And, if you are dissatisfied with any product or service for any reason, just return it to The American Homeowners Foundation for a prompt and full refund.

BOOKS
All books are $12.95 each.

LEARN HOW TO SELL YOUR HOME FAST!

Selling your home can be a traumatic experience even in the best of residential real estate markets. When the real estate market is sluggish, it can take longer to sell your home. But, with the proper preparation and planning, you can maximize the selling price and reduce the time your home is up for sale. Take the stress and worry out of the selling process!

How to Sell Your Home Fast! is 142 pages packed full of hundreds of tips, sample questionnaires, worksheets, negotiation techniques and suggestions to help you sell your home quickly and get the most from the asking price.

Weigh the pros and cons of selling your home without a real estate agent. Learn when professional advice makes sense and how to find the best qualified real estate agent for your home. Their are sample questionnaires for you to use at home to interview potential real estate agents and special questions you should always ask of their references.

Use the planning worksheets to develop your marketing plan. Check the tip lists to determine what publications you or your agent should advertise your home in and for how long. Check our special list of supplemental opportunities that can help you get the word out about your property as economically and inexpensively as possible. Learn to develop a promotional flyer on your home, what to include in it and when and how to use it to your advantage.

HOW TO SELL YOUR HOME FAST

Use the negotiation techniques to guide you through this tricky process. Learn the pros and cons of seller financing. Use the worksheets to walk you through the steps in analyzing the prospective buyer's ability to obtain financing for a mortgage.

BUY SMART! GET THE COMPLETE HOME BUYERS GUIDE!

Buying a home is one of the biggest investments you will make during your lifetime. So, you need to understand the entire buying process and your options in order to make the right decision. And, the right decision can equate to tens of thousands of dollars over time.

The Complete Home Buyers Guide is the book to help you understand and work through this process. There are dozens of exercises, worksheets and checklists to help you analyze your needs, your home requirements, your financial needs and tax status. Learn the pros and cons of home ownership. Understand how to qualify as a buyer for loans, mortgages and special financing. Learn how to negotiate the best deal for you. A Home Buyers glossary is included for reference to help you understand all the terms involved in the buying process.

LEARN HOW TO INVEST IN REAL ESTATE. LET THE HOME INVESTORS PLAN SHOW YOU THE WAY!

Real Estate is still one of the best investments that you can make. Almost anyone can buy real estate for investment. If you know how, you can buy smart. *The Smart Home Investors Guide* can help you become savvy and start you on the road to investment in residential real estate.

Learn how to make your investment property pay for itself while your equity in it grows. *The Smart Home Investors Guide* has exercises, worksheets and tips on analyzing your investment potential. Use the exercises to help you become an investor and to determine what real estate is a good investment for you. Work through the worksheets to learn the best way to structure your investment. Use the planning worksheets to assess the investment potential of a particular property. Use the tips to find yourself an investment bargain and where to go for loans. Read up on how to find a qualified agent to work with you. And, brush up on your negotiating skills.

MODEL CONTRACTS
All contracts are $6.95 each

HOME REMODELING CONTRACT

The American Homeowners Foundation and the Better Business Bureaus have received numerous complaints from homeowners regarding remodelers. A large share of the complaints can be avoided by making sure that both parties understand and agree in advance to all terms. The American Homeowners Foundation's *Homeowners/Remodeler Contract Agreement* is a six page sample contract document written in plain english describing the work to be done, completion timetables, payment schedules, responsibilities and rights of both the homeowner and the remodeler. This model contract can be used to increase your confidence in working with remodelers. A series of standard provisions have been developed from research done with homeowners, remodelers and the professional advice of architects, attorneys and contractors. Yours for just $6.95.

RESIDENTIAL SALES CONTRACT

Buying or Selling a Home? Even if a real estate agent isn't involved the buyer and seller will need a contract. The American Homeowners Foundation's Residential Sales Contract will fit the bill nicely. Don't miss critical points in your contract. Its six comprehensive pages cover the major issues buyers and sellers should always address in their agreement.

Buyers and sellers should both refer to this model contract even if real estate agents are involved. Buyers and sellers can use any contract form they want, and AHF's may have better provisions from the perspective of either or both parties.

For example, most brokers contracts call for the broker to hold deposits without any obligation to pay interest on the deposit to either party. The brokers may then put the money in interest bearing accounts and then keep the interest. AHF's contract calls for deposits to be placed in interest bearing accounts with interest to be paid to the buyer and/or the seller, depending on the outcome of their negotiations.

Be prepared with your own interests and protection in mind. Use the American Homeowners Foundation's **Residential Sales Contract** as a starting point to keep your best interest in mind.

Spend just $6.95 now and you may protect yourself from larger cash outlays later.

HOME CONSTRUCTION CONTRACT

If you're thinking about building your own home, you need a copy of the American Homeowners Foundation's model *Home Construction Contract.* This six page plain english contract was developed with the information homeowners, builders, real estate attorneys and architects. It is written to help you identify all of your costs, what you can expect from the builder, subcontractors, architects and your own responsibilities. This contract will help you prevent disputes or misunderstandings by describing what needs to be done, who is responsible and when each project is expected to be completed. It is yours now, just $6.95 during this special offer.

RENTING YOUR INVESTMENT PROPERTY

Use The American Homeowners Foundation eight page model residential lease and rental application to protect your investment property. Using it may help you avoid a bad tenant, a weak lease or other rental mistakes that could adversely affect your investment.

Its great companion to *The Home Investors Plan.* Yours right now for only $6.95.

OTHER PRODUCTS OR SERVICES

HOME SECURITY DECALS

Unfortunately crime is a growing problem across the entire country. Police departments consistently advise homeowners that you can help protect yourself, your family and your home from crime by discouraging criminals from trying to break in,

in the first place. AHF's home security decals will help in that regard. Place decals prominently on doors or windows where the criminal element will see that AHF's offering a reward for the arrest and conviction of anyone trespassing or violating your rights or property!
Help stop crime now for $7.95!

AMERICAN HOMEOWNERS FOUNDATION MEMBERSHIP

Membership in the American Homeowners Foundation provides members with valuable information, special advance notice and prepublication discounts on publications and services. Members also receive our quarterly newsletter *Homebase,* loaded with helpful tips and ideas for homeowners and prospective homeowners.

And as a new member, you'll get a set of three American Homeowners Foundation's home security decals to apply to your windows or doors. The decals protect your home by warning trespassers or vandals that you are serious about protecting your home. And they offer a reward paid by the American Homeowners Foundation for information leading to the arrest and conviction of individuals violating your rights or property.

The American Homeowners Foundation is a nonprofit educational and research organization. Membership is tax deductible as a charitable contribution.

Your contributions enable us to continue research, provide educational services to help homeowners, legislators and policy makers to learn about the challenges of American home ownership.
A one year membership is only $7.95.

Order Form

We are so sure that these items will help you that if you are dissatisfied with any product or service for any reason, just return it to us for your money back! It's that simple!

I. Books	Single	Qty	Order Total
a. ☐ How to Sell Your Home Fast	$12.95	_____	_____
b. ☐ The Complete Home Buyers Guide	$12.95	_____	_____
c. ☐ The Home Investors Plan	$12.95	_____	_____

SPECIAL QUANTITY DISCOUNT! When you order your first book, get an additional book for $9.95. When you order your second book for $9.95 get your third book for $7.95.

II. Contracts	Single	Qty	Order Total
a. ☐ Homeowner/Remodeler Contract	$6.95	_____	_____
b. ☐ Residential Purchase Contract	$6.95	_____	_____
c. ☐ Home Construction Contract	$6.95	_____	_____
d. ☐ Rental Application/Lease	$6.95	_____	_____

SPECIAL QUANTITY DISCOUNT! When you order your first contract for $6.95, get additional contract copies for $1.95 each. Special for contractors, investors and developers. When you order 5 copies of the same contract, your price is just $24.95!

III. Special Studies/Products/Services	Single	Qty	Order Total
a. ☐ Home Security Decals	$7.95	_____	_____
b. ☐ AHF Membership	$7.95	_____	_____

Shipping Charges	
Orders up to $8	$1.50
Orders $8.01 to $16	$2.00
Orders $16.01 to $24	$3.00
Orders $24.01 and over	$4.00

Subtotal _____

Shipping _____

Total _____

Method Of Payment

☐ Check or Money Order Enclosed for $ _____

☐ American Express   ☐ Discover   ☐ Mastercard   ☐ VISA

Card No. _____

Expiration Date _____

Signature _____

Telephone No. (_____) _____

Name _____

Address _____

City/Zip _____

For our information, how did you learn about the American Homeowners Foundation?

_____ 1. From newspaper, (which one): _____
_____ 2. From magazine, (which one): _____
_____ 3. From radio/TV, (which one): _____
_____ 4. Received brochure in mail.
_____ 5. From friends.

NOTES

NOTES

NOTES